| DESTROYING THE MASK | WHAT ABOUT THE CHILDREN? |

| Norlita Brown

Destroying the Mask: What About the Children?
Copyright © 2012 by Brown Essence, Inc.

L. Smith is the contributing writer to My Daughter, My Friend

BROWN ESSENCE, INC.
P.O. BOX 82462
CONYERS, GA 30013

Please visit our website at brownessence.com and let us know what you think.

Dedication...

I dedicate this book to my children,

Ve'Lynncia Jazzemin Morgan

&

De'Vray Camel Rogers

Their youth was stripped from them right before my eyes, and if I could turn back the hands of time, I would give it back to them on a silver platter.

Table of Contents

Foreword...

If the world was perfect, parenting would come with an instruction manual, every parent-child relationship would be blissful, and every kid would grow up to be a productive citizen. Unfortunately, our world is far from flawless, parenting comes with no guidelines, the relationship between children and their parents is often strained, and many kids grow up to repeat the mistakes of previous generations. When we were children, we vowed to be better parents than our own. Now as adults, we watch from the sidelines as our offspring lose their innocence to things in this world that only produce struggle, self-hate, and pain.

They say it takes a village to raise a child, however, the villages have turned into cities and within the inner city, community co-parenting is an extinct philosophy. There was a time when baby showers were given to expecting mothers as a platform for experienced women to pass down insight and encouragement. But how can we find wisdom when before we cut the cake and open the presents, we spend two hours avoiding the word "baby" and unscrambling words like bottle and diaper? Let us return to the former, putting away the silly games, and sharing knowledge that could keep our boys and girls from becoming the next statistic.

When I first heard of Norlita Brown's intentions to write a book of short stories about parenting, I was elated. Often the very people who need education regarding skills such as parenting refuse to take a course or read a nonfiction book about the topic. The beauty of creative writing is the ability to bring lessons to life and tuck pearls of wisdom underneath tales that entertain. This collection of stories inspired by real life situations has the power to awaken us from a state of complacency and cause us to recommit ourselves to being better mentors and role models for our youth. I urge you not to take these stories lightly, but to receive their truths and to pass them along to those who remain unenlightened.

Loving your children is not about giving them what they want; it's about giving them what they need. They need parents who are not afraid to say no, stop, and wait. They need adults who will hold them accountable and expect them to live up to their potential. They need mothers that will model self-respect and maturity daily through appropriate speech and behaviors. They need fathers who will express love and exhibit care just by being there. No amount of clothes, video games, jewelry, money, or any other materialistic item will replace a parent's presence and affection. Your child is not your friend, and should not refer to you by your first name. Your child is not your burden, and should not be reminded of how much they have ruined your life. Instead, your child is God's gift to you. He has entrusted you with someone He loves so much that He made them in His own image.

There are many parenting lessons that need to be learned and implemented if we are to save our children. Our young men are being weakened by mothers who coddle their sons instead of allowing them to develop a sense of autonomy and self-sufficiency. Our young girls are unaware of how they should act and be treated as ladies because of a lack of examples of healthy male-female interactions. Our kids grow up not understanding the nature of rewards and consequences because we overindulge them and are too afraid to be consistent with the rules we set in our homes.

When are we going to take responsibility for our hand in what happens to our children? In my experience counseling families, I cannot count the times parents waved the finger of blame at their kids for unruly behavior, completely unwilling to be liable for their own parenting errors. I cannot describe the stories I have heard about parents who are not proactive in resolving child academic, social or behavioral issues, but expect their children to come out of situations untouched and unaffected. This is not love; this is passiveness. Although your child may say you are the "coolest" parent now, their future is likely to be bleak because they are not gaining the tools required to survive and be successful in the real world.

Change is imperative and it begins with the decision to get honest and get real. Our children's futures are at stake, and we cannot afford to maintain the façade of happy homes when chaos threatens to rip our families apart. We can overcome the turbulence, but we must be willing to stop making excuses and start doing the work. It is time to see the beauty in our children and to give them the love we have always wanted for ourselves. It is time to reach out for help and stop pretending that we can do this all by ourselves. It is time to tear away the pretenses and allow the light to shine through. It is time to discard every idea that has set our children up for failure and that has kept us from soaring to new heights of humanity and freedom. It is time to destroy the mask.

A'NDREA J. WILSON, PH.D.
AUTHOR, PROFESSOR, AND
MARRIAGE & FAMILY EDUCATOR

Preface...

Children are blessings from God. This is a fact that many of us acknowledge. What we miss is how to care for the blessings that God has given us. Our world is filled with so many books that tell us the right and wrong way to rear a child, and as parents we understand that there is no perfect way, so we shake our heads to advice that doesn't fit into our circumstances. We turn our noses to the things that do not conform to our right now.

This book is for the little children. It's for the child who wants to play in the sand and not dance like she's 22 in a strip club. It's for the little girl who wants to wear ponytails and eat lollipops. It's for the little boy who wants to hold on to his pacifier a little while longer; the one who is not quite ready for potty training. It's for all the children who want to be exactly who they are, little children. Let's stop rushing our babies, pushing them to stages they're not ready for, because we want them to grow up so fast. We steal their childhood from them because them being children is hindering us from being adults. As long as they are babies, we can't go out at night and party, we can't hold two jobs. As long as they are babies, their lives are our lives so we push them to the next step, and sometimes we push them too far too fast.

This book is for the little children who at ten years old decide that the world would be better if they were not in it. What tragedy can happen to a child in ten years of being on this earth that would cause them to take their own life? Life is so precious and yet our children are living in a world where they are being taunted and teased, called names, driven to a point of insanity. Feeling hopeless at 10, 15 and 18 years old, they are tearing the world apart so that it becomes a reflection of the pain that they feel.

This book is for the parents, the ones who truly care. The ones who want to understand what happened to our children. I'm here to tell you that we are what happened to our children. We are the generation that took their childhood. We are the generation that changed the way that a child should go, and now it's time for our generation to make things right. To apologize for our wrongs, but more than that, admit that we were wrong. By that I mean, apologies are just words sometimes to many people, to actually admit that you are wrong is to believe, understand and take on the responsibility of the wrong that has been done and the damage that has become the result of it. I am that parent who felt like I did everything I could for my children. I felt that I gave them the things that I had and some of the things I didn't, but what did that mean to them, nothing. When they wanted me home, I was working two jobs so that they wouldn't have to live in a run-down neighborhood; so that there would always be more than enough food to eat; so their clothes wouldn't be handed down from anyone. I made a choice to give them everything but me. Trying so hard not to be like my mother, I wound up being exactly like her.

How did we lose our children? We lost them in so many ways. This book will prayerfully open our eyes to a few.

Introduction...

Right now, our children are becoming epidemics. Teenage pregnancy is at an all-time high. The shame that once came with being a mother at so early an age is now replaced with honor. In fact, it has gotten to a point where other little girls are disappointed if they are not having a baby.

Our young boys are filling up jail cells and detention centers. They are being labeled as incorrigible

I don't feel that I am a bad person, neither do I feel that I am a bad parent, but I do understand that I didn't parent correctly in many ways, and because of that, my children have suffered. We cannot recreate history, but we can make a change. The past is behind us, but the future is before us, and it can be so much brighter if we choose from this day forth to live a life that does not revolve around us, and instead revolves around our children.

I am not sure if your story is within these pages, but I know that mine is. I am not sure if you are ready to open your eyes, but I know that I am. So this is my plea. If you or anyone you know has children who are suffering, offer them this book, offer them your help, and give them your prayers.

As you read these stories, understand that each story in this book is a true depiction of my life or the life of someone close to me. However, I ask that you not take the focus from the purpose of this work by wondering which story is mine or that of another, because who they are doesn't matter what matters is the problems behind the actions. I ask that you approach this work with genuine sincerity and join with me to make a change for the lives of our children.

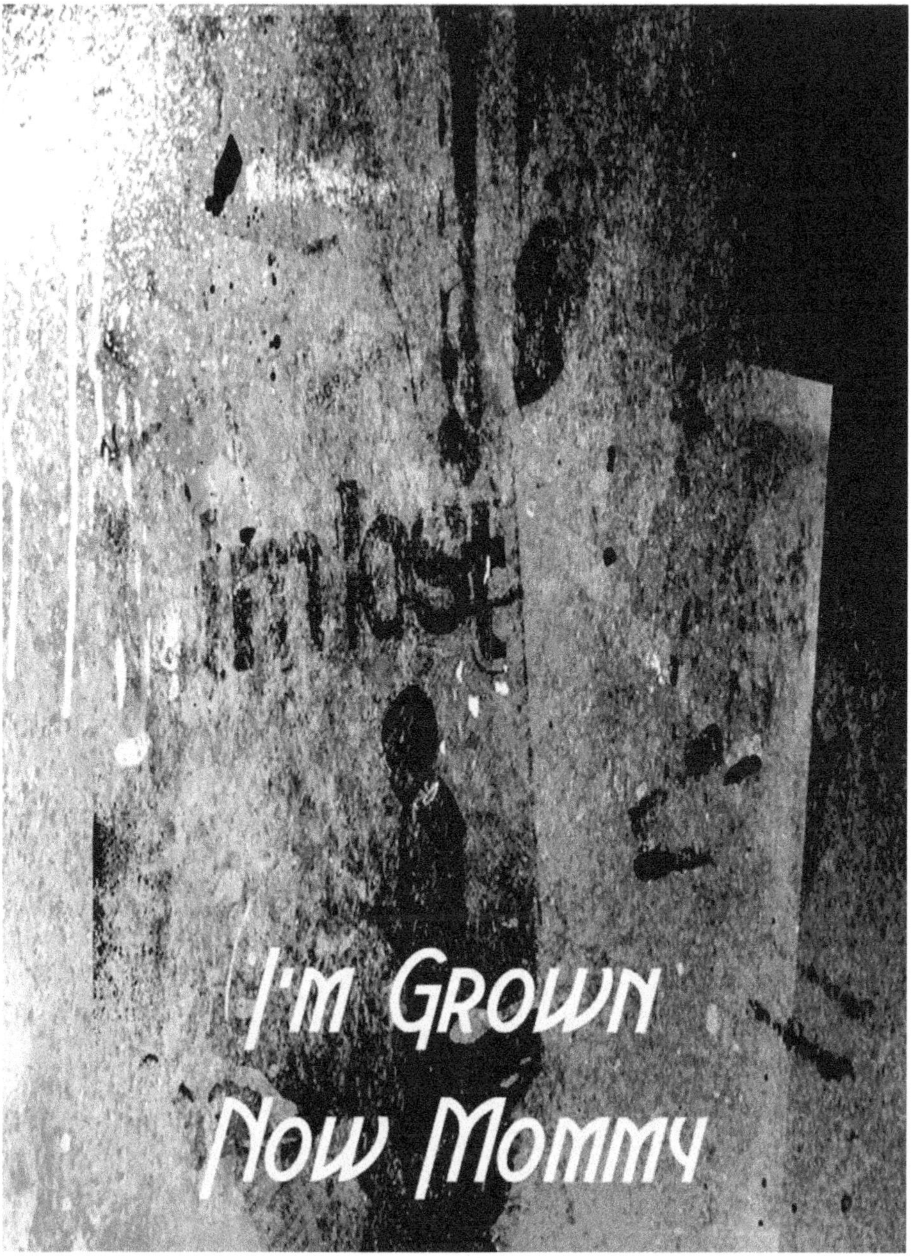
imlost
I'm Grown
Now Mommy

She was just fourteen years old. Her voice still held traces of her childhood. Her belly protruded with the hope of a baby she wasn't ready for. Her cheeks were still round, her body was not yet developed for her own years, and now it was being forced to develop another's.

"You're not grown," I said as I looked into her small brown eyes.

"But I am grown; I'm going to be a mommy just like you."

"Sweetie," I said as tears formed in my eyes, "you're too young to have sex, let alone a baby."

"How old were you when you had sex?"

I knew that she knew the answer. I wanted to choke on the answer myself. I was fourteen years old; God had blessed me not to carry a baby until I was nineteen, but even that was too young. She was born from my womb when I was twenty. "There are some things in life that can be learned by example and some things you have to learn on your own. My example is not a good one, not right now."

"So what are you saying?"

"I'm saying, I wish I had someone to talk to when I was your age, someone to tell me that I was too young to have sex. To tell me that love isn't about sex."

"But he does love me mommy, and I'm going to love my baby. We're going to be a family."

"What about your education?"

"Momma, I love you and I don't mean to disrespect you when I say this," she said as she removed the child-like

2

tone from her voice, "but honestly this conversation is too late. My baby is here now, there's no turning the clock back on that. I'm five months pregnant and I wouldn't have an abortion even if I wasn't. I'm going to have my baby. I'm going to love my baby."

As much as I didn't want to admit it, I had too. She was right. I wasn't asking her to have an abortion, that was the furthest thing from my mind, but I couldn't wrap my mind around the fact that my baby was now having a baby and there was nothing that I could do about it. All that I could do, I didn't. When she was letting her boyfriend in the house, I was at work. There wasn't enough money for babysitters. I had to work two jobs as it was to keep a roof over our heads. I did what I had to do.

Did you? I heard a voice inside me ask.

Yes, I responded, confident in my answer.

There were no other options? the voice asked.

No, I responded again with the same confidence.

How much were you making on your first job?

15 an hour, I said puzzled by the question.

And that was not enough to care for you and your children?

Not in a good neighborhood, I said, my confidence waning.

I see.

I let the calculations run through my head. My mortgage was right at $1,000.00 a month. My car note was another $300.00, the insurance on that was another $250. That didn't include the lights, water and gas bill; that had to

3

run me at least another $400 and those were just the necessities. What about the luxuries, the cable, cell phone and home phone, that had to be at least another $300. So what does that mean? We had to spend $2,250 off the rip before we even have food to eat or gas to put in the car to get back and forth, the clothes on our backs was a whole other story. Therefore, if I was making $2,400 a month before taxes, there's no way that would be enough for us to live comfortably. I had to work two jobs, I had to!

I looked at my daughters face, stared into her eyes as she was searching my face for answers. I was searching hers for the same. I rubbed her cheek and then I held her close. Tears began to fall as the revelation hit me. I didn't have to work two jobs. What I could have done was find a place that was within my budget instead of living above my means. I could have found an apartment for $600; or maybe even a house, the style wouldn't matter, but the fact that it would be a home would. I didn't have to buy a car. I could have taken the bus and saved up to buy a car that didn't come with a note. I could have. There was a lot that I could have done that could have made life much easier for me and my children. They would not have had to raise themselves while I went to work from work. I could have been home shortly after they got home from school. I could have helped them with their homework and cooked them a hot meal, but instead I chose to do me, all the while giving myself the excuse, the reasoning that I did what I had to do.

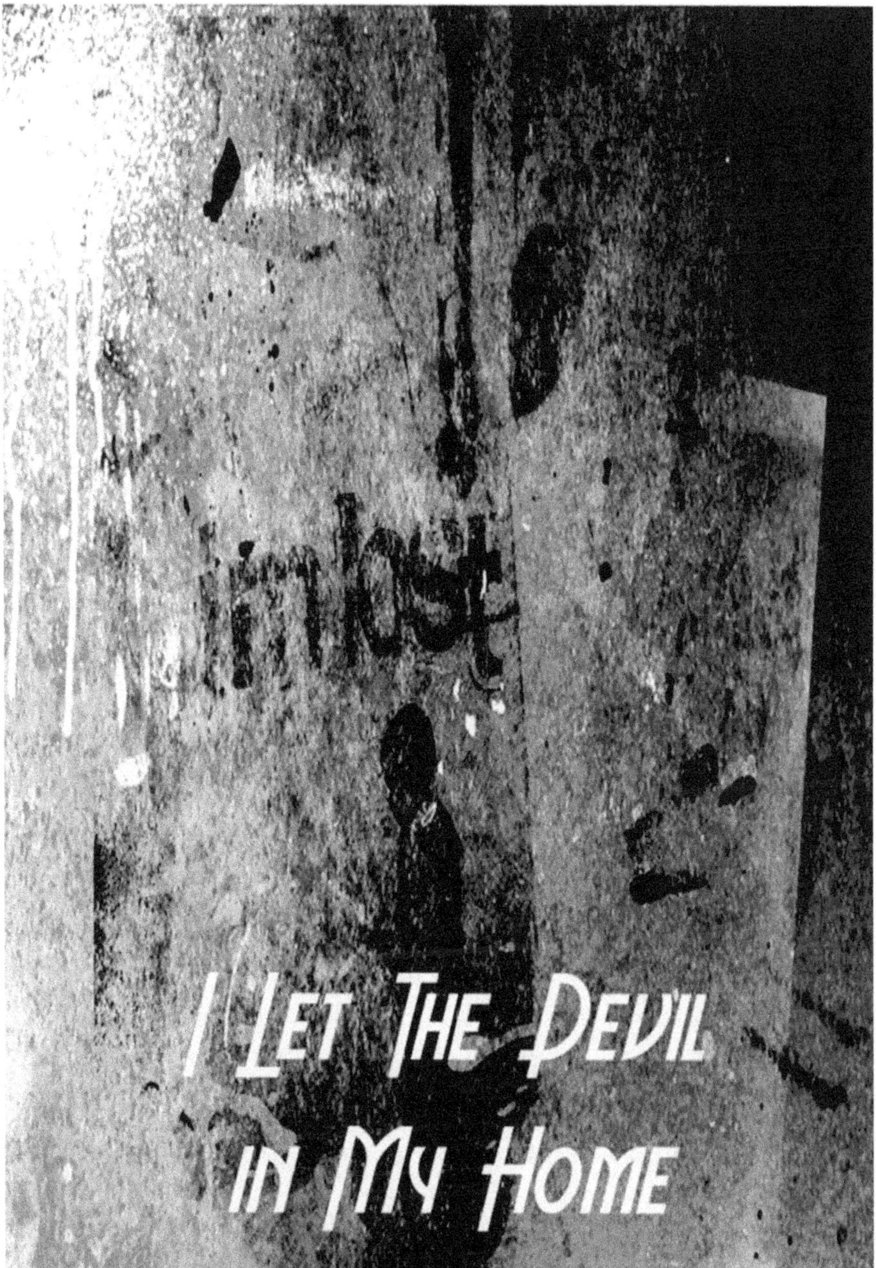
imlost
I Let The Devil
in My Home

I had made a promise to God and to myself that now was not the time for me to concentrate on men. I had been hurt too many times before. Now was the time for me to concentrate on me and my kids, Brianna, 7 and Bryan, 2. How quickly we forget the promises we make. I would love to say that I thought I was hearing from God, that He sent this man my way, but truth be told, I know now what I wouldn't recognize then. This man was a test and I failed miserably. I let the devil in.

We didn't have a car at the time so we were walking and bussing it everywhere we needed to be. Brianna and I had just taken the bus to drop Bryan off at day care. I was looking a hot mess. The only thing I was trying to do was get my children in place so that I could get ready for work. We headed to her school, walking. That's when I saw him, or he saw me, doesn't matter which; it was the moment that changed my life, literally.

He pulled his car alongside me and my daughter, and began to drive to the speed of our walk.

"Hello," he said. I turned ready to give him 'the don't bother me' spiel, well that was until I saw that he was better than fine. Don't get me wrong; I had some good looking men in my life, but this guy, no, none ever as fine as he was.

I am staring at his picture, trying to find a way to describe him; my description comes up short. I find that it is hard to describe him and give you the beauty that I saw when I looked at him. I stop. I wonder how important is it that you see what I saw, and I realize that it is very important, because to understand me, to understand this story, you have to understand everything. You have to know what I thought when someone who I never would have thought would give me a second glance stopped me, approached me and tried to throw game my way. His eyes were large almond shaped, they were a dark brown, but they looked so bright. His head was smooth and bald and his skin was very light. His lips were full and when he smiled he looked like he could be related to the Joker, but that did not take away from the drop dead gorgeous look he carried. His overall appearance would definitely put you in the mindset of Prince, The Artist. I could smell his scent from the car, he smelled like vanilla. It is a scent that my daughter still hates to this day, but we will get into that later on.

"Hello," I said returning his polite greeting.

"Do you need a ride somewhere?"

"No, we're fine." I mean he had me talking but I was no fool, I wasn't about to step into his ride without knowing him from Adam, and with my daughter, no doubt. No, I had to set some standards.

"That you are," he said and smiled. He put his thumbnail in between his tooth like a tooth pick and stared me up and down.

I returned his smile; the last thing I expected from him was a compliment. I mean, like I've already admitted, I wasn't looking my best, and even then my jaw would hit the floor if he dared to even look at me. I think this is where my downfall began. I never gave myself any credit.

I fed into what society had deemed me as and all my life. I was called names, told I was ugly, hell my own family confirmed this untruth for me. So, why would I believe any different?

"What's your name," he asked.

"Renee," I replied. "And yours?"

"Vaughn. So do you think I can get your number?"

I looked at him again, surprised by the request. I was twenty-seven, he looked like he was 18 maybe 19. "You're way too young for me," I said as thoughts of my sister's latest rendezvous played through my mind. She had just told me about an 18 year old that she was kicking it with and she is a year older than I.

"How old do you think I am?"

"I don't know, 18, 19 at best."

"I'm 32."

"Whatever," I said. He looked much younger than me, so I know there was no way in hell he was older than me. He pulled out his wallet and driver's license and I looked at his date of birth. "Wow, well you must take really good care of yourself."

"I try; you know the body is a temple."

"Are you quoting scripture?"

"I know the Word."

"Impressive."

"Why?"

"It just is. You just don't seem like the type."

"The type to what, know God."

"Okay, you got me."

I gave him my number; I refused to take his. I didn't trust myself. I wanted to leave the ball in his court. I didn't want to be hounding him, calling him way too many times, way too early. The tables were turned, and he did call me, in fact he called often. Unfortunately, the amount of attention he gave me had my face smashed down in the couch, letting him have his way with me in all of one week. I know what you're thinking, but don't judge me. I have already judged myself, besides I'm sure I'm not the only one who has been in this same situation. I'm sure many of you looking down at me right now have been here before, but that's not the purpose right now. You're getting me off track. I'm trying to keep it real, trying to tell my story, trying to let you know how I feel, how I felt.

Like I was saying, it only took a week or so for him to get into my pants, and two months later, when he told me he was moving to Atlanta, I admit it, I was heartbroken. That was until he asked me to move with him. I didn't care that I hadn't known him long. It didn't matter that my two year old son, kicked him the first time he laid eyes on him. Exactly, he just ran up on him and kicked him. If I had been more interested in a mother's intuition, I would have run then, but I didn't. I chalked it up, just like I chalked up the fact that my seven year old daughter didn't care for him either. She took a pen to his front seat. Rather than wonder what would cause her to do that, I scolded her for damaging someone's property.

I told my family, friends and co-workers the same lie I willed myself to believe. I wasn't moving to a state I had never been to, a place where neither I nor my kids knew anyone for some man. No, I was moving to Atlanta for my kids. I wanted to get them away from the mean streets of Detroit. I wanted them to be able to walk outside without the fear of gunfire, or all of the other dangers that were steadily rising in Detroit. As if none of this was happening anywhere else in the world.

The ride from Detroit to Atlanta was beautiful. We had left in January, right after Bryan's birthday during one of Detroit's worst winter storms. There was 10 inches of snow on the ground that looked and felt more like 2 feet, and as we got closer to the south, the snow just magically disappeared off the ground. Arriving in Atlanta, there were no signs of winter at all. My kids and I quickly shed our winter coats and got out of the car.

Vaughn had driven us to Decatur, GA. This was when I got the first hint that his invite had nothing to do with how he was feeling me, but more with the fact that he needed me. He couldn't move to Atlanta on his own. The lies he had been telling me were slowly unraveling. I wasn't as gullible as I was behaving, but I really wanted to make things work. Truth is, I was probably more of a sucker for his good looks and sex then I cared to admit, as I now think back on one of our earlier conversations.

"Is that your mother?" I asked, as I heard a distinct authoritative female voice in the background.

"Yeah," he answered in an annoyed voice that made me think twice about prying further. In fact, he sounded like a child being scolded.

"Is she visiting?" I asked inquisitively. He had told me earlier that he brought his mother a house in California. The fact that he was a barber driving around in a 10-year old Ford Escort should have been red lights blaring, STOP! LIES ARE FORMING IN HIS MOUTH! But I chose to take him at his word, chose to swallow the lies he was feeding me. He told me he owned the barber shop he worked in which made it a little easier to accept the lies.

"Naw, she needs to stay with me for a while," he said. His answer caught me a little off guard.

"So what happened to the house you bought for her?" Everything in me wanted to exit left as I watched the lies fall off his tongue like water off of a seal's butt, but then I remembered how gorgeous he was. I let wisdom take a back seat and understanding drive the car as I realized that no one wants to admit to being grown and still in their parent's home.

"She's renting it out; she missed Detroit."

I left the subject alone; it no longer seemed to have any importance.

"How much do you have?" Vaughn asked as he got back into the car. We had just pulled into the first apartment complex, and he was now holding the application.

"I don't know. Why? How much do we need?" I said refusing to play the only card I had. As much as I was feeling him, I didn't love him and I didn't trust him either. So to let him know how much money I was carrying was not gonna happen. At this point I was still under the impression that this was a joint effort and his money would match my money if not be more than what I had.

He stared back at me with a look that said he caught every point I was making and he was less than pleased with them. He didn't comment, he just quietly filled out the application. He didn't ask me for any of my information, so I assumed he was going to be doing this on his own. After several attempts and being declined at each one, we made a temporary move to an extended stay hotel.

To say that my children were unhappy would be more than an understatement. We had left behind a cozy home that we were renting to stay in a hotel for any period of time was absurd to them. It was to me as well, but I tried not to let that bother me. I felt like my life was slowly slipping out of my control, and yet I was determined not to run back to Detroit with my tail between my legs, showing my family and the world that I had failed. Failure was never an option for me before and I wouldn't let it be one for me now.

My scheduled interview was my last ray of hope, and yet, it did not go as smoothly as planned. The company that I was working for had promised me a slot in the Atlanta location, and that remained true, however what didn't was the fact that I would have to take a considerable decrease in my salary. I refused and went back to work for a temp agency. Atlanta was really not turning out to be a very good move.

I walked into the room; Vaughn had laid my light blue jeans with the matching long sleeved blue jean shirt on the bed. He was already dressed in the same outfit smiling uncontrollably.

"Okay, I'll bite. What's up?"

"I got a plan," he said still showing every one of his white teeth.

"I'm listening," I said hesitantly. Atlanta was his plan, so I was learning each day that his plans never really worked out so well. The kids were sitting with solemn faces staring intently at the television. Shame washed over me because I knew this was not what they should be doing at their age, so young and full of energy. I walked over to sit on the bed with them, they both quickly moved to the other side. I made my mind believe that they were just trying to make room for me, when my heart knew that they were really running away from me.

Although they were born from different fathers, they both owned beautiful bright eyes that seemed to look directly into your soul. It was these eyes that refused to look my way, refused to acknowledge that their mother had just walked into the room. I felt every bit of their pain, the only thing I knew to do was to keep trying to make this thing right, for them, for us.

I turned back to Vaughn who suddenly wasn't smiling so much anymore. "So what is this big plan you have?"

"Well, I used to clean windows, and I was thinking until we got something more solid, we could go clean a few windows to get some quick money in our pocket."

"That's your big idea. Why aren't you looking to get into a shop to cut hair?"

Vaughn did not answer he just stood there looking like a big kid who just had his dream crushed right before his eyes. "Baby, I know this is hard for you guys, but if you just let me fix it, I promise it will be worth it."

The kids turned away from the television for the first time since I had entered the room and stared at Vaughn in disbelief. My emotions mirrored their own as we waited for Vaughn to continue to tell us how he could make this right after encouraging me to uproot my family from a life of comfort to a life of living hell.

"Can we just try?" he asked with pleading eyes. I folded, went to the bed he had placed the clothes, picked them up, and headed to the bathroom to change. The kids stared at me knowingly, as if even at 7 and 3, they knew. They knew this was not the first nor would be the last battle he would win; he would have his way with us, with me. While I could only hope to one day understand the depth of the knowledge they knew.

We arrived at a small plaza that housed a few small businesses from beauty supplies to barber shops. Vaughn looked at me with excitement building in his eyes. I wanted to return the same hope, but I didn't have it in me.

"C'mon," he said as he prepared to exit the car himself.

"I'm not getting out," I replied as I noticed the smile fade from his face again.

"And why not?" he asked as he positioned himself in his seat, staring at me intently as if that would change my mind.

"I'm not a sales person, for one, and for two, who's going to be watching the kids while we're both out there hustling for windows?"

"We will be right here, they will be fine."

I refused to let him encourage me to abandon my children in a hot car, so I stood firm. Besides that, doing windows was just not my thing. "Look, Vaughn, I have a job. I'm out here for moral support and that's it."

"Fine," he said as he jumped out the car, slamming the door behind him. He snatched open the hatchback and started pulling his necessities out of the back. It was hilarious for me to see him continuously transform from child to man only to revert back to his child-like ways.

We watched as Vaughn went from door to door, searching for an opportunity to prove his plan correct. Each time he walked to the next door, I could see the hope draining from his every move. After, the 4th or 5th door, he finally had a bite. I could see his face light up, as he prepared to clean their windows. The barbershop was the one who had conceded. He moved the chairs from the window and spent a ½ hour cleaning the inside of the windows before coming outside and doing the same. Returning the chairs to their proper place, Vaughn disappeared for a few minutes. When he emerged, he was mad, storming back to the car, fast and furious.

He snatched the hatchback opened and piled his things back into the car, when he returned to the driver seat; I gently placed my hand on the back of his neck and tried to calm him down.

"What's wrong?"

"Nothing," he said as he started the car. I looked back at the kids who were finishing the snacks we had brought with us. I wasn't sure if it was wise to continue this discussion in their presence, but I didn't think it was best for Vaughn to be driving in this condition either, so I pressed on.

"Babe, I can see something's got you upset. Why are you giving up so quickly?"

"These people ain't tryna pay no money to nobody."

"Well," I began cautiously, "what did they pay you?"

"Nothing," he said as the anger began to build again.

"You can't let them get away without paying you anything. Do you want me to talk to them?"

"No, don't worry about it. I'll just figure something else out."

A small giggle threatened to make its way out. I tried to submerge it with more words; I needed to know what was going on. I wasn't surprised that his plan was blotched; it was rather far-fetched when I first heard it. I just didn't want to damage his manhood or his self-esteem, so I followed along.

"Vaughn, you just started. It can't be as bad as you're making it seem. What did they pay you, like twenty?" I knew that that would be a low figure for all the work that he had just put in, but I was trying to show him that it could be worse, until I heard the next words out of his mouth.

"No, they gave me $5.00 and said that my work wasn't all that good. Talking about he sees streaks in the window. That window looks ten times better than when I started."

If I could have stopped my reaction, I wouldn't have, it was hilarious. He had worked so hard moving chairs putting them back, cleaning the inside, the outside, and going over it again; all of that for five dollars. Laughter erupted from my gut. I laughed so hard. I cried tears like I was at a funeral. Needless to say, that only made matters worse because my laughter wasn't short-lived. It went on for at least five minutes. With laughter being contagious, my children began to laugh with me. I don't know if they realized why we were laughing or not, but everybody but Vaughn was holding their stomachs and wiping tears from their eyes.

Vaughn drove us back to the hotel room. I got up the next morning and prepared for my first day of work. The kids looked worried. I kissed them on their forehead and told them that everything would be alright. I shook Vaughn lightly, he opened his eyes and I told him that I was on my way to work.

"Work?"

"Yeah, I was trying to tell you yesterday, but you were too excited about your news for me to let you know what mine was. I should be back around 5:30."

"What are you doing?"

"Clerical for a temp agency."

17

"Where?"

"Can I call you with the details? I really need to get going before I miss this bus." Vaughn didn't offer to drive me to work, he just rolled back over and went back to sleep. When I called him later he told me that he was renting a booth at a barber shop in the flea market, and that the kids were there with him.

Vaughn called me again while I was on the bus ride back to the hotel.

"I had to give Bryan a spanking today."

"For what?"

"There's a room in the back with a television. So, I had the kids sit back there and watch TV while I was up front cutting hair. Well, Bryan kept pulling the plug out of the socket that was the electric source for the barber shop's television and radio."

"Uh, huh." I said listening and waiting for him to tell me why he felt the need to spank a 3 year old.

"I went back there and told him not to pull it out anymore, but he kept doing it, so after the 3rd time, I took him outside and whipped him."

"Okay, we'll talk about it when I get there," I said before disconnecting the call.

When I got to the hotel room, Vaughn had brought KFC and set it out for dinner. The kids face held the same solemn look they had when I left as they sat at the table preparing to eat.

I walked over and gave them my usual greeting and kissed them on their cheek. "So how did things go today,"

I said as I looked at Brianna. Bryan spoke very well for 3, but I wanted Brianna to tell me.

"Okay, I guess," she said as she pushed the mashed potatoes around her face.

"You guess? What happened?"

Brianna didn't answer; instead she looked up at Vaughn and back down at her potatoes. I took the hint and asked Vaughn to step outside for a minute. He made an attempt to protest, but thought better of it and stepped outside. He said he was going to the store and would be right back. When he left, I asked Brianna again how their day went. She remained quiet.

"You know you can tell me anything," I said as I knelt down beside her and placed my arm around her.

"Bryan got in trouble," she said quietly. I looked over at my son who looked heart broken.

"What did Bryan get in trouble for?"

"We were playing in the back and he kept tripping on the cord. Vaughn kept coming back there yelling at him and telling him to stop. I tried to tell him that it was an accident, but he wouldn't listen. When we left, he drove us to the woods, took Bryan out of the car..." Tears started rolling down Brianna's cheeks, now my heart was broken.

"He took Bryan out of the car and what, Brianna?"

"He took his shirt off, poured water on his back and took a stick from the tree and started hitting him over and over again. He was yelling at him. I got out the car and told him to stop. I told him he didn't mean it, but he wouldn't stop."

When I looked at Bryan, tears were covering his face too. I picked him up and tried to hold him close but he flinched as if he were in pain. I pulled his shirt up and what I saw made me gasp, my 3 year old son had warps and scratches on his back that was every bit the resemblance of slavery. My heart stopped as my tears now matched theirs. I sat them both in my lap and rocked them back and forth trying to comfort them from an ordeal they should never have had to face.

After a few moments, I went outside and waited for Vaughn to pull back up; I stormed over to his car and was met with his face full of tears.

"I'm sorry, Renee. I messed up, I know. I love those kids so much. I wasn't trying to hurt him; I was just trying to spank him."

"Vaughn, he's 3! What kind of spanking leaves him looking like a run-a-way slave?"

"I didn't know, you have to believe me, I didn't know. My grandmother used to get a switch to whip me all the time; I had no idea I was causing him that pain. I'm so sorry."

"I'm not the one you should be apologizing to," I said with my arms crossed in front of me. Vaughn nodded his head and went to apologize to the kids.

I know what you're thinking, because as I am telling you my story, I'm thinking the same thing. "Why in the world was an apology supposed to be enough? Why was he even let back in the hotel?" My answer is the worst possible answer there is, "I don't know." At the time, I was being very understanding of him rather than them. I did not believe that he meant to cause my son harm although he did just that. I did not believe that the abuse would continue and yet it did.

Only a week had passed before I would come back to the hotel room and find a black line under Bryan's eye. It was faint but it was there. With fists balled, I went at Vaughn, striking him everywhere my fists could land.

"It was an accident," he yelled as my punches were coming at him rapidly. Brianna and Bryan stared at the chaos that erupted right before their eyes. I never got an explanation from either of them about what happened to Bryan's eye. When my energy had decreased to a level that would not allow me to throw another punch, I sat down on the bed, winded.

"If you ever touch my kids again, I will kill you." I yelled. I had made my point, or so I thought.

I decided that the hotel room is what was making Vaughn so edgy and being with the kids all day under those circumstances wasn't making matters any easier. I called out of work the next day and Vaughn drove us to a young lady who kept children in her home.

We stayed with her the whole day, allowing the kids an opportunity to get comfortable with her and the other children she was keeping. Once I was satisfied that they were okay we filled out the paperwork for them to start the next day.

The fact that I was new to Georgia and had no sense of direction caused me to have a nervous breakdown. Well

I LET THE DEVIL IN MY HOME

maybe not exactly a breakdown, but it was very close. When I got off the bus to pick up my kids the next day, I had no idea how to get to them. I walked around in circles for over an hour before I sat down on the ground and just cried. It was another moment that made me hate the day I moved my family here.

After a half an hour, I called Vaughn who tried to direct me to the home to no avail. I hung up from him and called the lady assuring her that I was in the area and trying to find my way to her. She calmed me down and helped direct me to her home. When I finally got there, it was dark and I was visibly upset. I prayed that my children and I would find another means soon.

Things did get a little better for us because within a week we were blessed to get an apartment finally, after living in a hotel room for about a month and a half. There were children in the neighborhood for my kids, playgrounds and an afterschool program.

I enrolled Brianna in the afterschool program and placed Bryan in daycare. Things were looking up. They finally had a place they could call home as well as an outlet to play and make friends. Two weeks later I got a phone call from the school.

"This is she," I said into the receiver.

"This is Mrs. Jones, the assistant principal. I wanted to call you about, Brianna. Apparently she's having some difficulties."

"What kind of difficulties?"

"A few of the children have been complaining that she has taken their money."

"Okay," I said not sure what to say at this point.

"It's only been a dollar from each child, but we wanted to call you and find out if there are any problems at home that we need to be aware of."

"No, Brianna's fine at home," I said what I believed when my gut was telling me that Brianna wasn't fine. She hated Vaughn and she hated the move, but I kept praying that she would learn to love both. Every day her sad eyes were yelling at me quietly telling me that I needed to make a change for her and Bryan, and every day I just prayed that our situation would become comfortable for them without me making a change.

"Well, we needed to call and check. Also, if this behavior continues we will have to take further action."

"I understand," I said softly heartbroken that my little girl would even fathom stealing. "I'll have a talk with her when she gets home."

"That would be wonderful. We need parents that are willing to help rear the child; they are becoming a dying breed."

Not once did I consider the fact that I was a part of that dying breed because in my mind, I was there for my children. When I hung up the phone, I went to the kid's room. We were living in a two bedroom apartment and so the kids had to share a room. My heart dropped when I went into Brianna's drawer and found several dollar bills folded in various ways. She wasn't even trying to spend the money; it appeared that it was just a hobby for her.

Brianna, Bryan and I walked into the small apartment. Exasperated, I threw the keys on the dining room table and asked Bryan to go in his room to play. Kneeling down to meet her where she stood, I looked directly into Brianna's soft eyes, gathered her small hands into mine and asked…

"Are you okay, Brianna?" She was now 8 and although I suspected she understood the depth of my question, the innocence in her age gave her the way out.

"I'm fine," she said as she looked at me puzzled.

"I got a call from your school today," I said as I stood and walked into the kitchen to prepare dinner. Brianna followed, but she made no comment. "It seems that there are a few children missing money and they believe you are the cause of it."

"I haven't stolen any money," she said as she crossed her arms in front of her and stomped her little feet.

"Brianna," I said as I leaned back on the kitchen counter, "I saw the money in your drawer."

"Why were you in my room?" she questioned as if she had a right to. That disturbed me.

"Brianna!" I said sternly, "You don't question me; now answer my question."

"You didn't ask one," she said becoming more defiant by the moment. I wanted to snatch her up and shake her, but I thought better of it.

"Okay, where is the money coming from?"

"My friends, they're giving it to me."

"Why would they give you their money, Brianna?"

"Because they want me to be their friends."

"Brianna," I said as I knelt back down to meet her where she was. "What you're doing isn't right. You have to stop taking money from these kids. The principal called and she said they would be taking action. You don't want to go to jail do you?"

Brianna looked at me as if she didn't believe a word that I was saying, but she answered, "No, Mommy."

"Okay then, so no more taking money."

"Okay," she said as she put her head into her chest. I wanted to grab her and hug her tight, but I grabbed her hands and shook them gently instead.

"Go do your homework."

Vaughn got home later than usual. I didn't even care to know what had kept him. My day was long dealing with Brianna so I really didn't want to take on his issues. I did decide to share what was happening with Brianna with him.

"There was a little girl in my class when I was growing up who was behaving the same way. Her grandmother cut her hair off."

"Why would she cut her hair off," I asked as I sat up in the bed staring at Vaughn in utter disbelief.

"She said that she was concentrating on the wrong things. That she thought she was too cute and if she didn't have the hair then she wouldn't think like that."

"That's absurd."

"It worked. She came to class quiet as a mouse and didn't do nothing but her work."

"I can't see doing that to Brianna."

"Her hair will grow back, Renee."

I laid my head on pillow and closed my eyes but I did not go to sleep. I no longer wanted to have the conversation, but his words and Brianna's actions kept me awoke most of the night.

Vaughn had been coming home later and later each evening. I would ask him about his whereabouts and he would always have some lame excuse or another. For all the work he was doing cutting hair, he never had money to help pay for any of the bills. According to him, he only made enough money to cover his booth rental and gas to and from work. I often wondered if that was the truth then what was the point. Tonight was another night he was late. The phone rang from a number that I didn't recognize.

"Hello,"

"Is Renee there?"

"This is she."

"You don't know me, but I'm a friend of Vaughn's."

"Okay," I said really not caring to have this conversation.

"Well, I just wanted you to know that he's unhappy with you and that you're stressing him out."

"I'm sorry, who are you?"

"Oh my bad, my name is Tangie and I work at the club. He be coming in here talking about you and how he not happy and things, and I just thought I'd let you know. You know, woman to woman."

"Uh huh, so what y'all sleeping together? Is that what you're calling to tell me?"

"Oh, no. It ain't even like that. We just friends."

"Okay, so what is it like then."

"I mean, I'm just saying."

"You haven't said anything."

"Well, he said that y'all moved here from Detroit with yo kids and that y'all be causing him all kinds of problems. He said that he trying hard to stick in it with ch'all but you be making it difficult and things."

"Okay, Tangie. I appreciate your call." I hung up the phone. I wasn't sure what the purpose of her call was and I really didn't care. I was pissed that she had the audacity to call me for whatever reason. As soon as Vaughn entered the apartment, I went at him.

"Who is Tangie?"

"I don't know. I don't know a Tangie."

"She called here and seemed to know you very well."

"Is that supposed to mean something to me?"

"Shouldn't it?"

I went over the conversation that I had with Tangie blow by blow with Vaughn who didn't seem fazed the least. He didn't look like he had just got caught cheating at all. I remember thinking 'he's good.'

"Let's call the number back," he said confident that it would work out in his favor.

"Can I speak to Tangie?" he said as he placed the phone on speaker.

"There's nobody here by that name."

"Does somebody there know Vaughn?"

"I'm the only one here, and no, I don't know Vaughn." I couldn't be certain but it did not sound like the same lady that I had just spoken to. I looked at the number that Vaughn dialed and confirmed that it was the same number that had just called me, it was. Still, once he disconnected the call, I called the number again and asked for Tangie myself only to get the same responses Vaughn had just received.

Vaughn jumped in the bed and turned his back to me, apparently satisfied that this conversation was over.

I threw a pillow at his head and said, "Oh no, you don't get out of it that easy." You would have thought I threw a brick at his head as he jumped out of the bed quickly and got into my face.

"Oh so what, you're going to hit me?"

"Don't be throwing pillows at me," he said as his face turned a beet red and he huffed like he was a bull with smoke coming out of nostrils.

I threw another pillow, Vaughn charged at me. I swung and started landing punches. Once I saw that I had the better of him, because he obviously wasn't a fighter and probably didn't expect me to fight him, I jumped on him. I was choking him, scratching him and hitting him without care. When I was done I told Vaughn he had to leave.

"I'm not going anywhere; this is my place just like it's yours."

"Like hell it is. You have not once paid a bill or put a dime to the rent. You're leaving here tonight," I said as I tried to catch my breath from the fighting.

"I would love to see you try," he said as he went into the bathroom to investigate his wounds.

I picked up the phone and dialed the police. I told them that I had just been beat by my boyfriend and I wanted him to leave my apartment immediately.

When the police arrived, I repeated what I had told the operator earlier.

"Can I see your wounds?" the officer asked.

"I don't have any," I said slightly caught off guard.

"Sir, can you step outside with me?" the officer said to Vaughn and I felt relieved that we were making progress.

That relief would be short-lived, about 15 minutes exactly. When the officer returned to the apartment what he said to me had me floored, he read me my Miranda rights.

"What are you doing?" I asked as he began to turn me around and place handcuffs on me. My heart was racing, I started sweating.

"Mr. Walker has decided to press charges."

"Charges? For what? He beat me."

"Unfortunately the bruises that he has sustained tell a different story."

"Wait, I have my children. They're sleeping, why would you arrest me?" Now tears were falling as I tried every avenue I could think of not to go to jail.

"Can they stay here with Mr. Walker?"

"No, they're scared of him," I admitted the truth that I always knew, but it wasn't for their advantage it was for mine. I was praying it would keep me out of jail, it didn't.

"Well, we can have a social worker pick them up."

"Oh my God," I said as I thought of a way to make this right. I didn't want my children in the system, but I didn't want them staying there with Vaughn alone either. Besides, after telling them that they were scared of him, that was no longer an option. They let me ask the neighbor if she would keep them, thankfully she agreed and I was carted off to jail for the first and last time of my life.

It was a Friday evening and the judge wouldn't be able to hear my case until Monday. It was the longest 3 days of my life. I literally felt like I was doing hard time and would never see the light of day.

Vaughn was in court when the judge heard my case. He agreed to drop the charges and the judge ordered me to an anger management conference. Vaughn drove me home in a van that I had never seen before.

"Where did this come from?"

"It's my cousin's. She loaned it to me so I can move my things out of your place."

"So you're leaving?" I asked with mixed feelings.

"That's what you asked me to do."

"Yeah, but I wish I didn't have jail time to make it manifest."

"You hit me remember."

"With a pillow."

"It still hurt."

"That's because you're a wuss," I said before turning to face the window. I just wanted to get back home to my kids. Vaughn was working my nerves. I was glad that he agreed to take me home because I didn't have another way, a fact that he understood clearly.

Needless to say, the children were ecstatic that Vaughn was leaving. Unfortunately for them, he was only gone for a few months before he came back with his tail between his legs, wanting us to try again, and the fool that I was let the devil back into our home.

I told myself that I was just helping a friend in need. In fact, for the first month or so that he was there, he slept in the living room. I was dating other people and had begun enjoying life without him, but it wasn't long before I wanted him to return back to the bedroom we once shared.

Vaughn's reappearance also brought back the reappearance of the folded dollars. The weeks would come and go, yet it was rare that I would not find the folded dollars on Brianna's person, hid in her drawer somewhere or coming out of her clothes when I was doing laundry. It felt like my daughter was slipping slowly out of control and I had a front row seat. I had warned her of Vaughn's threat to cut her hair off if she didn't stop, but even that fell on deaf ears. I never got another phone call from school, so I was praying that meant that I had time to correct the behavior before Brianna got caught again.

Although her school didn't call, the next call I received was just as bad if not worse. It was Mrs. Tina from the afterschool program.

"I was walking back in my office when I saw Brianna taking money out of my desk. We had been having problems with someone taking money out of the children's book bags, but we didn't know who it was. Unfortunately, after this incident, I tend to believe that Brianna has been the culprit on the other occasions, too."

"I'm sorry."

"You may want to look into getting her some counseling, maybe the move was too much on her and she's having a hard time adjusting."

"Yeah maybe," I said as I listened to her words with no intent of sending my daughter to a therapist as if she was crazy. I did, however, decide to concede to Vaughn's insistent request of cutting her hair as discipline.

Tears were in her eyes as well as mine as she screamed and pleaded, "Please Mommy, don't let him cut my hair." She ran into my arms and cried so hard my heart melted.

"Brianna," I said as my tears joined hers, "I have been asking you time and time again to stop stealing and you won't."

"I'll stop now, I promise, I will."

Now a mother with compassion would have listened to her child's plea. Unfortunately, I was not that mother. I was fed up; I didn't believe she would change. Further, I felt if I didn't follow through on the discipline that I had warned her I would do, she would never take me seriously again. These are the thoughts I filled my mind with as I reasoned with myself that I was doing what was best for her. I took Bryan and headed out the door, leaving Brianna home alone with Vaughn unable to witness the devastation that we were causing her.

Vaughn had taken Brianna to his barber shop and cut her hair off. When I got home, the long pony tails that she had when I left was replaced by a very low afro. I was floored, I didn't know what I had expected, but this wasn't it.

Brianna looked at me with hate in her eyes, little did she know, at that moment, I hated myself too. I called family and friends and told them of the events that had unfolded, praying they would offer sympathy on my behalf; none was given because none was warranted. They were all appalled and hurt for my daughter. I was as well and all the reasoning I had fed my mind earlier didn't seem to justify the action now.

DFACS (Department of Family and Children Services) called me on my cell phone while I was at work the next day. They told me that they had been informed by my daughter's school that her hair had been cut. The worker went on to tell me that it was child abuse and they needed to schedule a meeting to come into my home and evaluate their situation.

"Hello, Mrs. Thompson. I am Mrs. Dawson from DFACS, can I come in?"

"Yes," I said as I stepped aside to let her in. "The children are still in their after care programs, should I go get them?"

"No, that won't be necessary. I have already spoken to them," she said casually as she made her way into our small apartment and sat at the dining room table.

"Okay," I said cautiously as I sat across from her.

"Let's talk about Brianna's haircut."

"What do you want to know?"

"First, what would make a parent, especially a mother, cut their daughter's hair?"

"Well, Brianna had been stealing money from other children."

"Let me stop you right there," she said, "my question was really rather rhetorical, hoping that you saw how insane it was to cut a young girl's hair the way that you have. The bottom line is this, there is no reason that you could tell me that would allow me to say, okay, I see your point. So in essence, what you have done is abused your child."

Fearing that I was now at a point of losing my children, I decided that my answers would be either, 'yes or no'.

"Do you understand what I'm saying?"

"Yes."

"It is our recommendation that you take parenting classes. They will be held at this location," she said as she

34

handed me a flyer. "We are also recommending that Vaughn is removed from the home until he takes parenting classes, as well as anger management classes."

"Okay."

"If you do not take heed to our recommendations, we will proceed to having the children removed from the home. It's in their best interest," she said as she smiled like she was giving me good news.

"I understand," I said as I walked Mrs. Dawson to the door.

Vaughn stormed around the apartment screaming profanities, staring at my children and me as he packed his bags. He had refused to go to the parenting classes or the anger management, but either way he had to leave the home.

I was heartbroken. I couldn't believe that our family was being torn apart. Tears flooded my face as I looked at the situation unfold. Then I did it, I did the unimaginable, I looked at my daughter and said words that seared right through her heart. It is funny how we react in situations so quickly that we never think about the damage they may cause to anyone. I looked at her sad face of eight years, having recently been traumatized with a haircut no little girl should have had and this being the result of it, I screamed at her.

"You tore our family apart."

"You see what you did," Vaughn chimed in, "you have your mother crying. Are you happy now?"

Brianna ran into her room crying as if the words we spew at her, shattered her fragile heart. And if I was to guess, I would say they probably did.

Looking back on the relationship now, I can't say that I ever loved Vaughn or considered him to be a real part of our family. I honestly believed that I just loved what he offered, the idea of a family. I have to also admit that the idea of him being a part of our family and being what I considered gorgeous didn't hurt matters. My mother thought the world of him. Every time I called her with issues about him, she would sing his praises. Now, don't get me wrong, I'm not trying to shift the blame; I am trying to open the door of understanding.

This understanding is not only for your benefit but for mine. If you knew me, you would know that I usually think with a sane mind and make rational decisions, so I look over the pain and hurt that has literally been a constant in my and my children's life for quite some time, and I am constantly wondering how I let such a chaotic and destructive lifestyle continue for such a long period of time.

Unfortunately, this was not the end; in fact this was only the beginning. There would be more abuse. I even suspected him of molesting both Bryan and Brianna.

I know you're wondering if I will close this story without telling you our end. Well, I almost did, but I owe you that much. Vaughn and I didn't end our relationship with me opening my eyes and understanding that my children needed me more than he did. I would love for that to have been the case because perhaps then they would find the road to forgiveness a little easier. This is how things ended with us.

It was a trip back to Detroit. I was excited that I was working a job that allowed me to finance a trip for all of my nieces and nephews to Cedar Pointe, a popular amusement park in Ohio. There were so many of us, ten to be exact. The teenagers broke off and did their own thing, but that still left Vaughn and me with two different age groups to split. He took the five to ten and I took the rest. I gave him their spending money and we parted ways.

When we met back up the kids that were with Vaughn was complaining about being hungry, I asked why they hadn't eaten. They went on to tell me how Vaughn had used their money to feed himself. He brought them one drink to split, between three young kids. I was heartbroken, but more than that, I was tired.

We drove back home to Detroit; I was arguing and fussing the entire time. In all of my spewing and stewing, I knew one thing. Vaughn and I were no longer. I left him at my mother's house as Bryan, Brianna and I drove back to Atlanta, never to look back on that relationship again. He arrived at the house with a U-Haul about a week later; I had already placed all of his items in the garage. He packed up the U-Haul with his belongings, placed the key on the table and left.

Now that you know my story, I wonder if you will make the same mistakes that I made. Will you put a man before your child, your children? Will you always assure them that their well-being is far more important than his understanding? Will you walk down the same road as I and let the devil in your home?

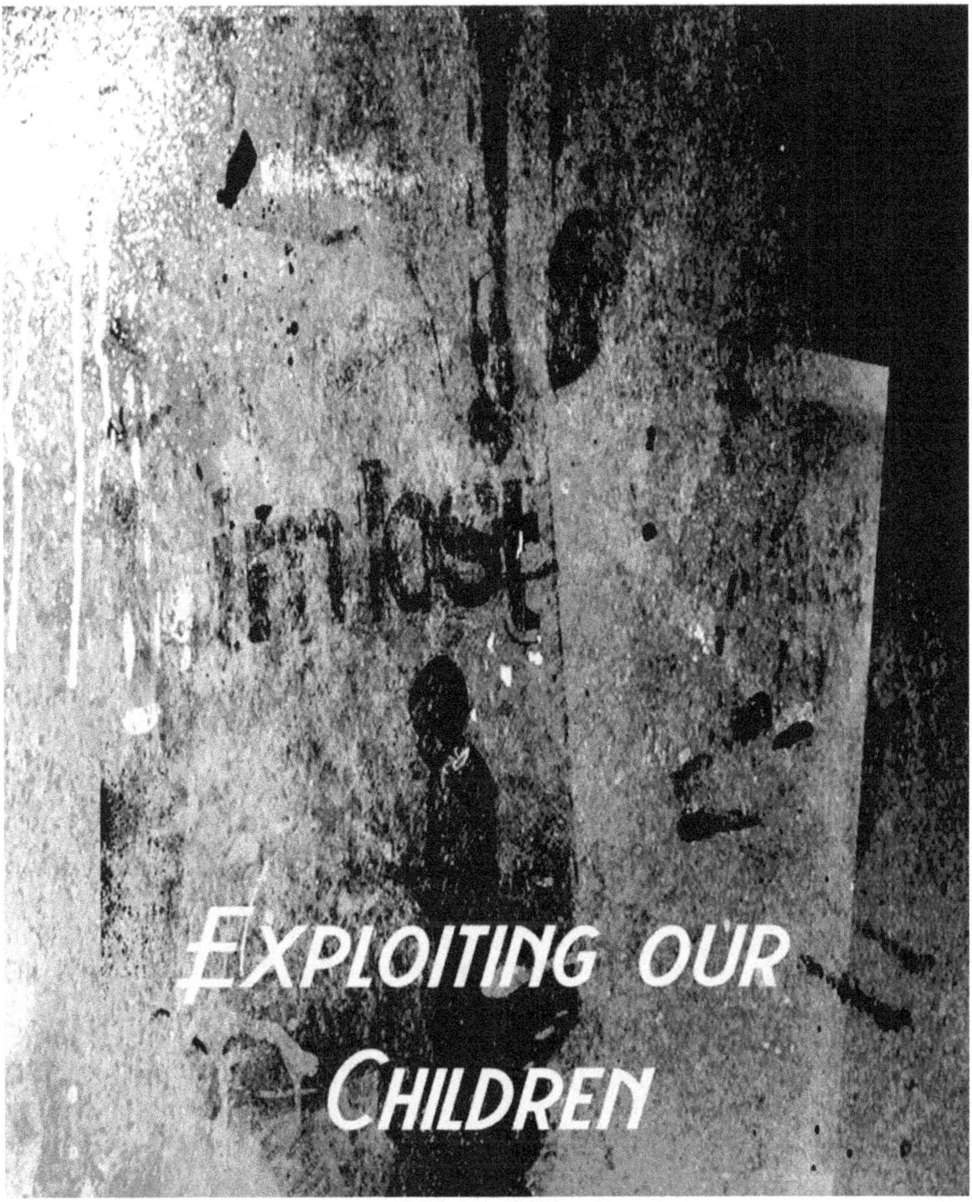
imlost
EXPLOITING OUR CHILDREN

"Whatchu think about this?" she asked as she held up a mini skirt, that to me would not have been cute for any age, but this was made worse because it was designed for a three year old little girl.

"I don't think anything about it," I responded casually, I didn't want to have a conversation about what I really thought.

"You don't think Ciara would look so cute in this?"

"Uhhh, no, I don't." Ciara was Tasha's three year old granddaughter. She had the cutest dimples on the softest brown skin and big round brown eyes with eyelashes that batted so innocently. She was a doll.

"You're just a hater," she snapped as she picked up another mini skirt and half top set.

"Please tell me how can I hate on a precious, three year old little girl?"

"Cuz, you know she would be cute in this, but you over there tryna play her short."

"Okay, look Tasha, I really wasn't trying to have this conversation with you, but you are just really trying to go there. There's a mirror over there for you to see who really is playing Ciara short."

"Oh no you didn't; see that's why I don't like hanging around your boogie behind."

"Oh so now I'm boogie because I think it's inappropriate for a three year old to be wearing a mini skirt and half top."

"She's three! It ain't like she's 18; then I can see you having a problem with what she got on. Shouldn't nobody be looking at no three year old like that."

"Exactly, so why would you dress her like that and bring attention to her like that. She is a child and should dress like a child."

"Duh, we are in the children's section."

"I'm done with it, Tasha. Whatever you want to do, you're going to do; so do you boo."

That was the end of the conversation that went absolutely nowhere. Tasha purchased both outfits along with a few other pieces that were too old for Ciara's young age.

Even after our little spat, Tasha invited me to Ciara's birthday party. She was having it at a small park close to her home. I was glad to see that Tasha didn't hold anger for long, and happy for the invite, or so I thought. When I got there I saw that Ciara was wearing one of the outfits that Tasha purchased the day we were shopping. The skirt stopped right where her underwear did, and with Ciara being so young, she was not cognizant of the fact that every time she bent this way or that way, her underwear was exposed for the world to see.

I shook my head sadly, and yet before I could digest this exploitation, Tasha was turning the music up on the latest adult club song. I wondered what happened to the nursery rhymes and other songs that were created for the children. Ciara was playing in the sand trying her best to make sand castles. I went and sat in the sand with her.

41

"You can play," she said with the sweetest most innocent tone.

"Thank you. What are you making?"

"I dunno; maybe a castle."

"Okay, are you a princess?"

"Yes," she said. I was enjoying the conversation with Ciara. I loved the fact that despite her surroundings she was still enveloping the life of a kid. It took my mind off the club music that was playing in the background.

Tasha came and grabbed Ciara by the hand. She was recording the party and had the camcorder in the other hand.

"Come on, Ciara," she said. "It's your party, you have to dance."

Against my better wishes, I walked over with Tasha and Ciara. Shame washed over me as I wished that I could gather all the little kids and just run with them. Little children from 3 to 10 were dancing provocatively as the adults cheered them on.

Tasha guided Ciara to the center of the circle and cheered her on, "Do it, Ciara. Look at Reyna," she said referring to another little girl who had her legs gaped open as she shook her butt like a dancer in a strip club. Ciara mimicked the little girls dance.

After a few minutes, she asked Tasha, "Can I go play in the sand now?"

To my dismay, Tasha asked her to continue to dance. I walked away. There were no words for this situation, and I could no longer stay and be a part of one of the many ways we become a detriment to our children.

Tasha and I kept in touch, but friends we no longer were. I'm not so sure that we ever were. I ran into her years later.

"Hey," I heard her familiar voice say as I turned around.

"Hey, Tasha, how are you?"

"I'm good. What's new with you?"

"Nothing much; how's Ciara doing?" I watched as Tasha's face became solemn.

"She's fine. She's a big girl now. You know she turned 18 last month."

"Wow, no I hadn't realized so much time had passed. So what is she into now? Is she in college?"

"No, she got herself a little job at the club."

"Oh, she's a waitress." The tone and disposition that Tasha had told me that she was dancing at a strip club, but I wanted Tasha to make it clear.

"No, she's dancing," she finally said as she turned her head away from me.

"Congratulations!" I yelled excitedly, raising my hand to give her a high five.

"Girl, stop. What are you congratulating me for?"

"That's what you were training her up to be and she made it! I know you're happy."

"No, I was training her up to get an education so she can make something of herself."

"I'm going to have to disagree with you, but it's cool if that's what you believe. I want to say this, there's nothing wrong with dancing, if that's what you have to do, but Ciara didn't have to do that. She could have and still could do so much more if you encourage her in the right direction.

"The blessing is," I said as I continued to give Tasha the spiel that I should have given her so long ago, "she didn't wind up in the hands of a pedophile or a rapist. We are damaging our children's self-esteem. We are placing them in the wrong hands, the wrong places. There was a time when it took a village to raise a child, now if you say more than two words to a parent then you're out of line. So, I should have said this a long time ago, but I'm saying it now. Stop being instrumental in our kids becoming a negative statistic, and do everything you can to helping them become a positive one."

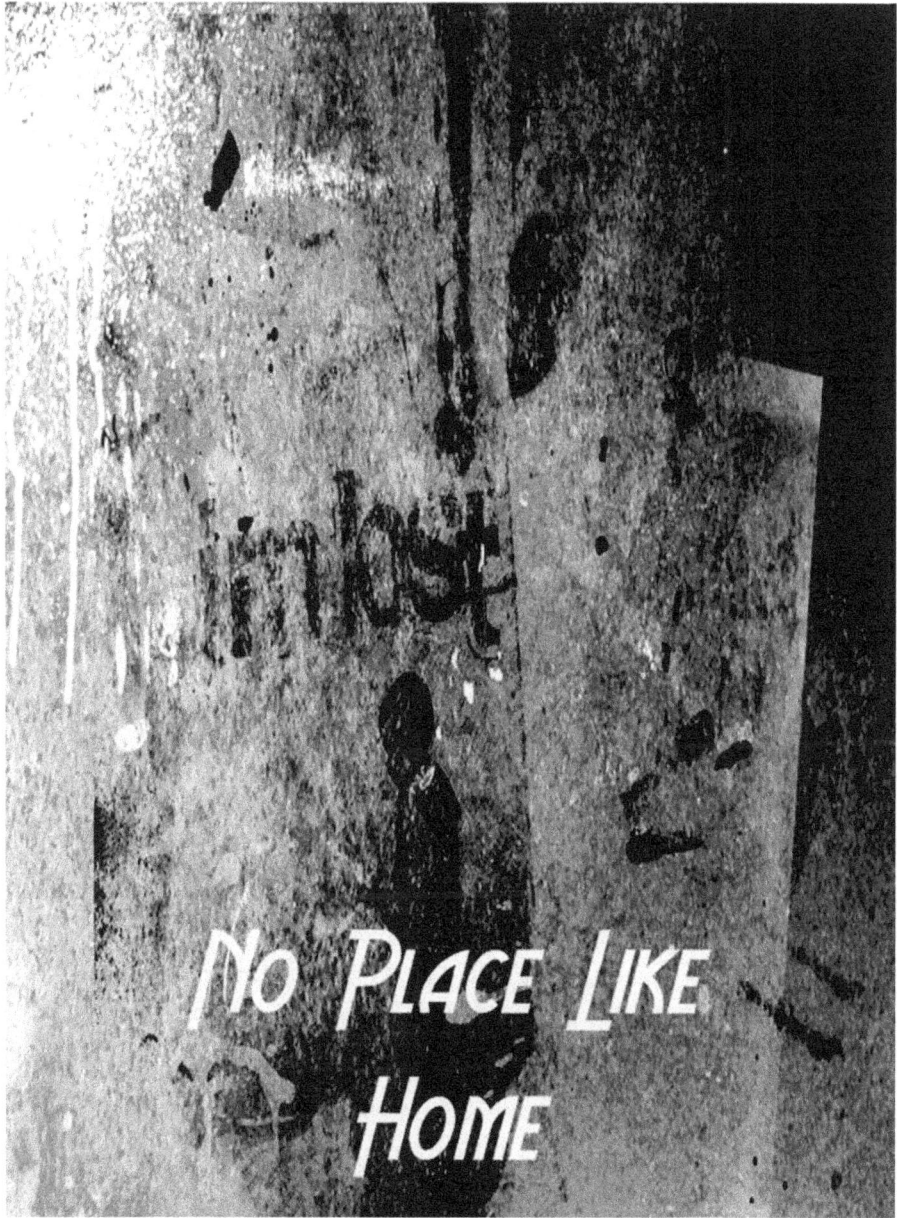

He stormed around the home making demands and screaming profanities. She stared at him, slightly afraid of him and for him. He was her precious baby of fourteen years. She didn't know what had turned him into the monster that she was witnessing. Just moments ago she had asked her son to take the trash out. She expected him to grab the trash and take it to the curb. She didn't get what she expected.

"You want the trash out, you take it out. You ain't doing nothing."

"Tre' who do you think you're talking to?"

"Look," he said as he stood from the couch, his 6'2 frame seeming to tower over her petite 4'9. "I don't see nobody else in this room but you, Ma. You asked me to take the trash out; I'm saying I don't want to. Now I'm done with the conversation," he said as he stormed out leaving her standing in shock.

She shook her head as she went to grab the trash and take it to the curb. She was tired of fighting with Tre'. It seemed the older he got, the worse he got and she wasn't sure how much more of it she would take.

When she came back through the door from taking the trash out, she heard Tre's music blasting throughout the house. The obscene language violating her ear drums, her morals. She walked up and banged on his door.

"What!" he screamed as he snatched his door opened. Clothes both clean and dirty were strewn across the floor haphazardly.

"Turn that music down and clean this room up," she said as she stared into his eyes, the scowl on his face making her feel like she intruded on his space.

"Is that all?" he said, and she was glad that he didn't disrespect her again.

"Yes," she said and turned to walk away. The music lowered. It was still a little too loud but she was just glad that he had turned it down some. She didn't want to ruffle his feathers by returning to his door again.

Hours later the music was still playing in full force and Tre' had been slick enough to increase it again. It was well after his bed time. She went and knocked on his door again. There was no answer, she opened the door and saw that Tre' was knocked out sleep lying across his bed. He hadn't bothered to touch his room like she asked.

She saw dirty dishes on his nightstand, his dresser, and even a few under the dirty clothes that were on the floor. She went to the stereo and turned it off. Tre' jumped up.

"What the hell?" he said noticing his mother in his room. He stared at her like she was in serious violation.

"I knocked, Tre'" she began in her defense. "You didn't answer so I came in. Why haven't you cleaned this room like I told you?"

"It's in progress," he said as he lay back down and went back to sleep. She shook her head wondering at what point had their relationship turned into this. She turned his light out and closed the door quietly behind her.

His eyes were bright and beautiful. He reminded her of an angel. He was so smart and intelligent that she was so proud of him. At 3 years old he could hold a full conversation. His vocabulary seemed extensive and he was a quick learner.

She smiled every time she watched him mimic someone else. It amazed her how quickly he could pick up the demeanor and characteristics of a person. Sometimes this proved to be a little embarrassing as well. Tre' had just cursed. She wanted to pretend that she didn't hear the vulgar language come from such an angelic face, but all the eyes on her made it impossible to avoid.

"Tre' what did you just say?" she asked praying that he wouldn't repeat the word.

"Nothing," he said as he held his head down. She was relieved that it seemed he was feeling the shame from his statement. Though the gawking eyes of her family members told her she shouldn't be done with this conversation yet, so she pressed on.

"Where would you learn such language from?"

"From you," he said without batting an eye. Shame now filled her face as she tried to quickly correct him.

"Tre', we don't tell lies. You probably got it from that music your dad listens to with you." She knew that her statement didn't make the situation any better, but at least some of the weight was shifted off of her right now. Well, that was until Tre' shrugged his little shoulders.

"Okay, but y'all tell lies too," he said with the innocence of a three year old. She knew that she could no longer continue the conversation in every one's presence. There was no telling the degree of embarrassment she

would obtain if she continued this way. She got up and grabbed him by the hand, walking him into another room. She didn't discipline him though; there was nothing she felt that he had done wrong. He was only three.

"Tre'," she called out as she looked at the alarm clock, telling her that once again Tre' would be missing his bus and be knocking on her door requesting a ride to school. She couldn't understand how he kept missing his bus. It was a privilege and convenience that his school bus stop was directly in front of their home. Yet it was a convenience that Tre' refused to take full advantage of.

She couldn't remember the last time he had ridden the bus to school, always relying on her to get him to school. It angered her at times because she felt that he was taking her for granted. Fueled by that anger, she threw the covers off of her and slid her feet into her cozy slippers. Winter was quickly approaching and the cool air served as its confirmation.

She grabbed her robe from the bedpost and threw it around her quickly. Snatching the door open she stormed down the hall. When she arrived at Tre's door, she banged hard. She felt like the warden or better yet the police. Tre' opened the door half naked. He had his bottom wear on, but his chest was exposed.

"Damn, Ma. What's up?"

"Watch your language, TreShawn," she warned.

"What's up?"

"You are! You're about to miss your bus again and I'm not taking you to school anymore."

"Then I guess I won't be going."

She squinted her eyes tight as she glared at her only son. "Try me!" she said as she stormed back down the hall she had just come from.

True to form the bus pulled up as she watched every child but her own load onto the bus. "Tre'" she shouted back down the hall, "you're missing your bus."

The bus driver blew her horn for last minute passengers who may be running behind in their home. Tre' still had not appeared. She walked down to his room and swung his door open; she didn't care about giving him the respect of knocking. Tre' was sitting on his bed watching television with the windows wide opened. If he was trying to air his room out, he failed. It reeked of marijuana.

"I know you're not bold enough to smoke in my house and while I'm home."

"I don't know what chu talkin' 'bout."

"Tre', I can smell the weed, stop playing me for stupid."

He stood and turned the television off, grabbed his book bag and headed toward the door.

"You just missed your bus."

"Damn, so you gone take me?"

"No, I'm not. You're going to walk and you better watch your mouth."

Tre' walked back to his bed, threw his bag back on the floor, cut the television back on and lay down. His life and hers flashed before her eyes as she quickly contemplated her next step.

"I'm not playing with you!" He said as he poked his five year old chest out like he was a grown man.

'That's too cute,' she thought as she watched him imitate other men he had seen. He walked over and stood right in front of her. He grabbed her hand with his small little fingers and she smiled at how precious his little hand felt in hers.

"Come on," he said looking serious. "I'm not playing with you," he repeated.

He wanted her to make him something to snack on. She was waiting for the commercial to come on. She was so engrossed in the show but this little cutie pie was waiting for no one. She huffed as she stood to follow him into the kitchen and prepare his snack.

She frowned at the thought. Everything that she believed was so cute, no longer was, but now he was fourteen years old and she found herself daily counting the number of years she would legally be required to provide for him. The second he turned eighteen she would have his bags packed and at the front door.

She didn't care where he was going or how he was getting there; the only thing that she knew was he had to go. She placed her hand on her stomach as the pain hit her that she had created everything he had become. Now, she was throwing up her hands in surrender.

She walked back to her room and dialed 911.

"911 what's the nature of your emergency."

"I have an incorrigible son who is refusing to go to school. Do I have to go to court or can you send an officer."

"How old is your son, ma'am?"

"Fourteen."

"We'll send someone right out."

She was relieved that they took her situation as serious as she did. She threw some clothes on quickly and waited for them to arrive. She went back down to Tre's room and glared at him. She didn't know if it was possible to hate her own child, but she was beginning to believe that was the exact direction her feelings for him were heading.

He turned and glared back at her, and then he got up from his bed and closed the door in her face. She clenched her jaws tight. Yeah, she was more than fed up.

The officer arrived and she was happy that he looked intimidating, praying this would get Tre' going in the right direction. Unfortunately for her, Tre' didn't cower easily so it took a little more coaching from the officer than she had hoped, but when it was all said and done, Tre' was walking to school.

He didn't speak to her when he arrived back home from school that day. Anger still traced the outline of his face as he looked through her then past her, heading to his room, turning his stereo on blast once again and shutting his door tightly. She sighed as she sifted through the mail. She never expected Tre' to still be angry, but he left her no choice in the matter.

Over an hour had passed with no word from Tre', she made her way up the stairs and knocked lightly at his door. He didn't answer. She knocked a little harder, still no reply. She opened the door, Tre' was fast asleep on the bed. She walked over and tapped him lightly on the shoulder.

"What?" he yelled as he pushed his shoulder back causing her to jump for fear of him swinging on her.

"I'm about to make dinner. Are you eating?"

"I don't know. I doubt it."

"Tre'," she said with a small giggle and a smile hoping that she could lighten the tension that was so thick in the room, "You have to eat something."

"I'm not hungry; now can you please leave."

He had said please. Although she wasn't happy with his tone, she felt like it was a start in the right direction. It would be weeks before he would speak to her again, but he didn't miss his bus one day in those weeks.

"He's going to be the death of you?" he said to her as he stormed across the bedroom fuming from his latest scuffle with Tre'.

"You think I haven't uttered those same words? What am I supposed to do?"

"You're supposed to parent! You're supposed to be his mother and put aside being his friend! One thing's for sure, you're definitely not supposed to oppose discipline!"

"I'm not opposing discipline; I'm opposing abuse!"

"Did you hear the things he said to me? What he thinks is okay to say to an adult! He's twelve and he is

making my life and yours a living hell. It's not his fault though, I blame you."

"Don't you dare go there?"

"Oh, I dare. You're living in a fantasy world if you think he is going to just magically turn out to be a good man when you baby him, allow him to do and say whatever, and for what?"

"You don't understand," she said as she turned away from him. She couldn't look at him or face his truths. She knew she was taking Tre' down the wrong road fast but what she didn't know is how to stop the drive.

He walked up to her and turned her back to face him. "You have to stop blaming yourself. His dad leaving him is not your fault and no amount of babying is going to make up for that."

Tears ran down her face at his understanding, she was trying to make up for the fact that his father wasn't around. She found herself constantly letting things that Tre' did slide because she felt he already had enough to deal with. His father left when he was three and from that point on it became she and he alone, facing the world and its ugly trials and tribulations. She just didn't know when it had gotten so far out of control.

Sweat dripped down her eyebrow; she reached up and wiped it away with the back of her hand. She looked around Tre's room making sure that she wasn't leaving anything behind. Satisfied, she picked up the last box and headed toward the door.

Tre' walked in startling her so much that she almost dropped the box in her hand.

"Yo, whatchu doing in my room, Ma?"

"Moving a few things out," she said as she tried to walk past him but he blocked her way.

"You ain't taken my stuff," he said in aggressively, angrily. She dropped the box. "If anything in there is broke, you paying for it!"

She moved closer to him and grabbed his shirt into a bunch. She pulled him closer to her face with anger etched deeply into her mask.

"I'm going to say this one time! Things are changing as of today! Your attitude, the way you think you can talk to me, all of that is moving in a different direction. If you step to me wrong one more again, I promise you it won't be pretty."

Tre backed up from his mother, shock on his face. "Oh, so what you just gone abuse me like your boyfriend!" he snarled, his lips curled tight.

"He didn't abuse you and neither will I, but discipline is about to take a front seat here. Tre' you're going down the wrong road. In a few years, you will be old enough to leave home and you're not ready for that world out there," she said with a lightened tone trying hard to reach her son.

"How 'bout I do us both a favor and bounce right now?"

"How about you act like you're fourteen and I am your mother not your step stool? You don't have a choice to live anywhere but here, don't try me, Tre'."

He walked past his mother, into his bedroom and slammed the door shut. She turned around opened the door back up without knocking. He looked up at her with hate in his eyes. She stared back at him with scold in hers.

"You will not slam another door around here either. If you slam this door again, I'll take it off its hinges." She shut the door quietly, picked the box up and walked down the hall. One step at a time.

We have a choice with our children. Often times we make mistakes that we live to regret, but we must first understand that we don't have to live with that mistake. We can make changes in our lives, in the lives of our children as long as we remember it's never too late.

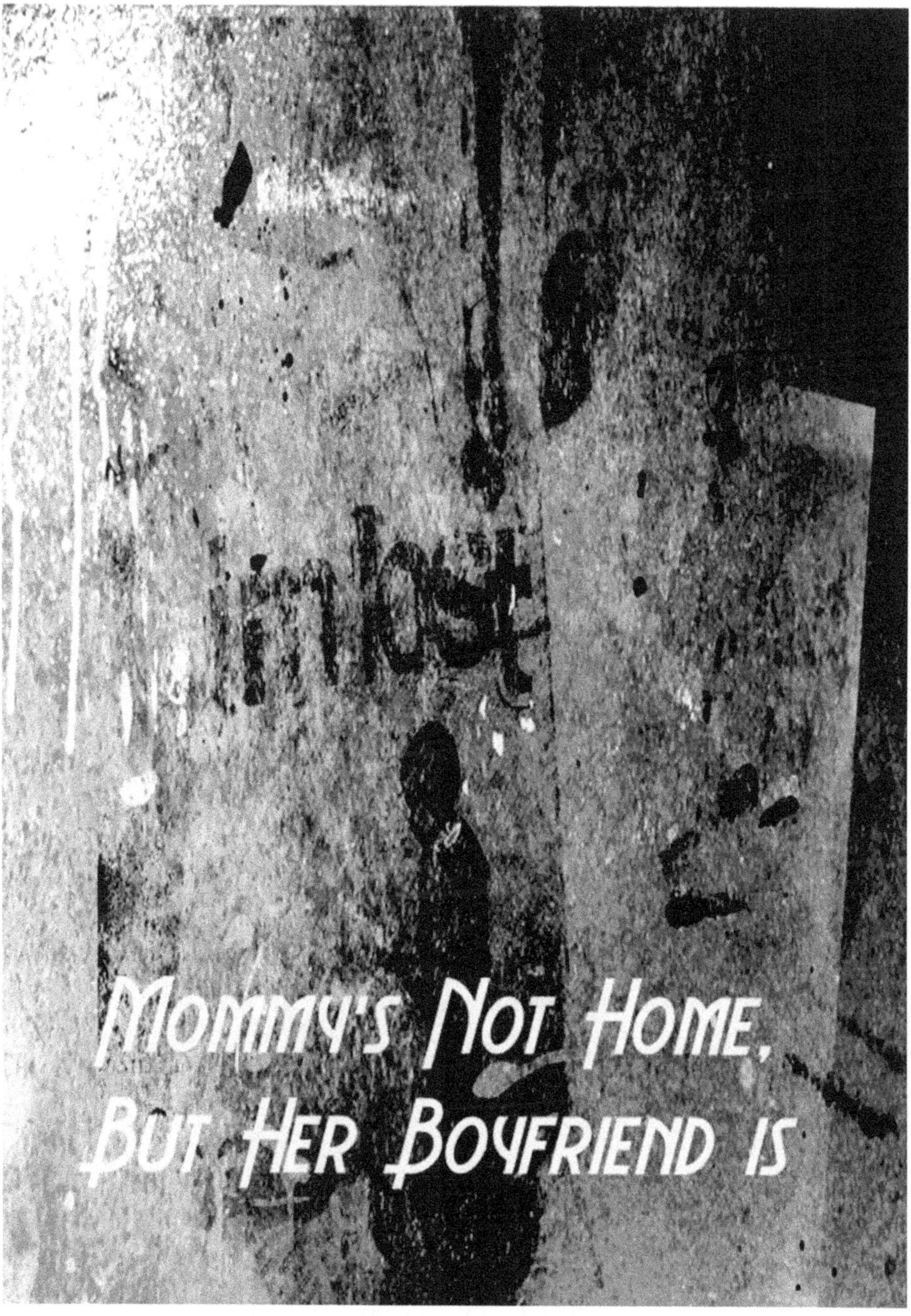
Mommy's Not Home,
But Her Boyfriend is

My memory tells me I was thirteen. He was so handsome with long wavy hair and a muscular physique. My sister and I would comment on how gorgeous he was and giggle. So imagine my surprise when he told me that I was beautiful.

He was lying on my mother's bed when he called me to him. I stood on the side of the bed wondering what he needed.

"Sit down," he said motioning to the edge of the bed. The bedroom door was open; my sisters were in the next room. I would have never guessed that anything would transpire that could be considered wrong. I sat down. He grabbed my hand gently.

"I see everybody comes around here for your sisters, but I want you to know that I think you're beautiful."

I held my head down in shame, "No, I'm not. I'm the ugly one just like they said."

He sat up, placed his hand under my chin and lifted my head up. "You're the prettiest one to me."

I smiled, no one had ever told me I was beautiful, never said I was pretty, and now for the first time I was hearing these words from someone that both me and my sister thought was gorgeous. My smile widened. I felt like Celie from *The Color Purple*.

I stood to walk out, but not before hearing him say, "You definitely got the best body." Now that I knew was true. At thirteen, I had a Coca Cola bottle shape. If I had nothing else, I at least had that. I walked out smiling from ear to ear. Oblivious to the fact that a seed had been planted, and just like the apple in the garden, it should have never been touched.

My oldest and baby sister had lives. They were never home and neither was my mother. She would be working one job or another and sometimes she would be taking classes. That left me alone with him many times. I don't remember what he said, I do remember that the compliments turned into outright flirtation and I was flattered.

I remember my oldest sister losing her virginity and telling me how she bled on the sheet. I remember wanting to see if that's what would happen to me. We were alone; I was in the den watching television when he came in. He sat next to me and kissed me before telling me to lie down. I did; I was ready to lose my virginity to a man who was not only twenty-two years older than me, but he was also my mother's boyfriend.

When he was done, he got up and walked out. I jumped up from the couch in search of the blood that was the mark of my virginity. I found nothing; I searched and searched to no avail. There was none. I hung my head in disappointment feeling cheated by life again.

When I came home from school a few days later, he called me into my mother's bedroom. He was nude; I knew what he wanted and I was willing to give it to him. I got in the bed and let him do what he wanted to. As odd as it was, I now considered my mother's boyfriend, my boyfriend, too. My mother came to me later that night asking me how my earing wound up in her bed. I smiled inside knowing that I was the other woman. I shrugged my shoulders as I took the earring from my mother.

If my memory serves me correct, these two incidents would be the only two occasions that I would sleep with my mother's boyfriend. Yet, it wasn't because I felt any remorse or that I felt a certain obligation or respect for my mother. It would be because I would, like my mother, stay up and wait for him to come home. Looking out into the dark streets, I would wonder if he would make it home in time for us to have sex.

By the time that he was ready to have sex with me again, I had finally had my own boyfriend. My first love, Anthony Myers would sit on the phone and talk with me forever. He would tease me about being a virgin; of course I no longer was, and I would very honestly tell him so. He would ask me who I had sex with since we went to the same school and lived in the same neighborhood, we knew all the same people.

Of course I could never confess who the person was; I couldn't humiliate myself like that. I fell in love with Anthony fast. He was the only boy who had ever paid me any attention and it was exciting. So when my mother's boyfriend called me to the basement and tried to get me to have sex with him, I refused. I was no longer his. I had moved on. He was extremely upset. I was confused and told him so. I spoke from the reason of an adult as I told him that what we were doing was wrong and should have never happened in the first place. He knew it was because of my boyfriend that I was no longer willing to have sex with him, and he was right.

Weeks had passed, maybe even months. My mother's boyfriend had tried once or twice to get me to change my mind, but I wouldn't and so he stopped asking.

Now we are all there in my mother's bedroom. My mother sat on her bed with her best girlfriend. My oldest sister stood next to me, my baby sister and her friend stood on the other side. My baby sister's friend was confessing at my sister's encouragement. She told my mother that her boyfriend had tried to have sex with her.

My jaw dropped just as my mother's did. My oldest sister was the only person who knew that I had sex with my mother's boyfriend. She pushed me lightly on the shoulder in encouragement, willing me to speak my truth too. I did, but it wasn't received well at all. My mother told me that I was a liar and that if I wanted to continue my lies then I would have to find another place to live.

Where would I go? I was thirteen years old. I told my mother she was right, I lied. We would never revisit this subject again in life.

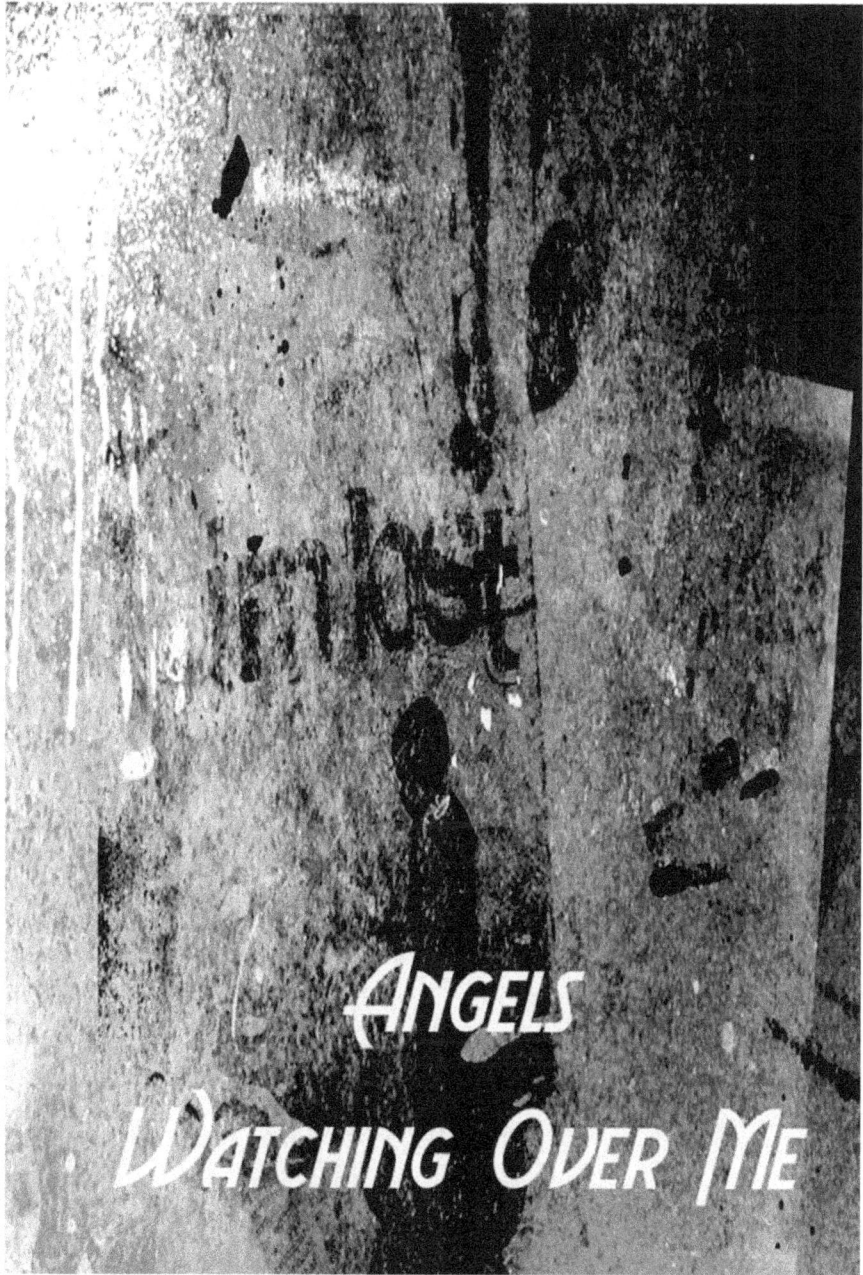

If I had a choice, I would have never designed my face this way. I would have chosen to look like her rather than him. If I had a choice; I would have never decided to have short hair or dark skin. If I had a choice, I would make me over to be the one that she will love, they will love, because it seems who I love is the one person no one loves.

Running from the buckle of the belt, I slid under the bed praying that she wouldn't hit me again. As I felt the sharp metal cut into my head, I instantly knew that I was wrong. I woke up in the hospital room at five years old getting stitches in the wound that my mother had given me. Every day, I woke up knowing that my mother hated me. It was a feeling of discouragement. I knew it was because I looked like my father. I'm sure you're wondering how I could know such a thing.

Well, she told me. Every day that she could, she would say, "You look just like your damned father and you know how I feel about him." Yes, I did know all too well that she hated him, and I had been cursed with his face, staring at her every day reminding her of a cheating lover, a broken heart, a damaged marriage.

I carried this hate to my baby sister who was born from a different father. So she became the child my mother always wanted. I stared at her with her light skin and long beautiful soft hair. I envied the love that was showered upon her effortlessly. Everyone wanted to know her, be her, claim her.

I was seven, she was three when I was ironing my clothes and she stood at my side constantly telling me it was her turn to iron her clothes. I wasn't finished, I kept telling her, but she kept insisting. I granted her wish, though not in the form she wanted it in. I took the hot iron and placed it on her chest, burning her clothes and searing her skin.

I don't recall whether or not she had to go to the hospital, but I do know that she had been marked for the first time with the hate that had been building in me. I always adored her; she is now and was then so adorable that you had to love her. Yet, it seemed every time that I tried to move in the direction of loving her, my mother gave me another reason to hate her.

I can remember a time on Valentine's Day when my sisters and I were at my grandparent's house; our ages were 11, 10 and 6. My mother came in to give my baby sister a huge box of chocolates, teddy bear, and a card to wish her a Happy Valentine's Day. My oldest sister and I waited in anticipation to what our gift would be, only to find out that it would be nothing. It was one of the many revelations that in our mother's mind, our baby sister was better than us.

There was the occasion when as sisters tend to do, my baby sister and I traded, and she wore something of mine and I in turn wore something of hers. The moment my mother laid eyes on me in my sister's gear she went ballistic. She yelled at me saying, "You better not ever let me catch you in her clothes ever again!" I protested and told her it was a swap. I don't recall her exact words, but the gist of it was, my baby sister can wear whatever she wants, but I was not to wear anything of hers.

Graduating from 8th grade with honors would prove to be a significant date in my mind for many reasons. I walked the stage proudly as they announced my achievements as I looked out into the audience trying to capture the looks of my family's faces. Surely my mother would be proud of me now. I looked over the crowd and did not see a family member in sight.

Naturally, I assumed that this could only be the case because of the difficulty seeing through a sea of faces from the place that I stood. However, when the graduation ended and all of the graduates went to their perspective families, brimming with love and hugs, I remained the lone person walking around to no avail. It was then that I realized what I already knew; no one had made it to my graduation because my baby sister was graduating that same day from 5th grade.

I made the forty-five minute walk to my sister's school and joined my mother, aunts and uncles who were all in attendance there. I smiled as my baby sister crossed the stage. She came down and hugged me and I her. I knew it wasn't her fault. She was oblivious to the pain in my heart that not one person thought it would be okay to come to my graduation. My high school graduation went even less celebrated. I can remember begging my mother to wear one of her dresses to my graduation. "You can't fit anything of mine," she said. I knew this too, but I also knew that I didn't have anything else to wear either. It wasn't for lack of money either. My mother simply didn't care to celebrate my achievements. After much pleading, she agreed and I searched her closets the entire night settling on a black dress that was way too big for me.

My mother wouldn't make it to my high school graduation, but what upset me was the fact that they had sent her the picture of me crossing the stage. It would be a picture that I would never get to see because she "misplaced it" once she saw it. My graduation from college would be the first and only graduation that my mother would attend of mine.

Turning thirteen is significant to so many youth because now, you are officially a teenager. My oldest sister and I celebrate our birthdays five days apart. I remember how excited we were that our mother was actually interested in what we wanted for our birthday since I don't recall many if any time that she ever celebrated the day. We showed her the bike that we wanted in the toys magazine, excited at the possibility.

Our birthday is in July while my baby sister's is in February. So imagine my excitement when the bike that we wanted was there waiting. I was slightly taken aback because there was only one. I just assumed that my oldest sister would be getting hers on her birthday in five days. I was wrong; the bike was for neither one of us. It was for my baby sister.

So yes, my mother started a war within me that transferred to my baby sister. It was one that would continue for years, with my baby sister having no knowledge of why our relationship was so strained. She loved me and I loved her too, but that love was nothing in comparison to the resentment that I had that was a direct effect of the difference that lay in my mother's lap.

My oldest and baby sister both were blessed to look like my mother. I admired their beauty and though I looked like my father, I once thought that I too was beautiful. Until, I was taunted and teased by my sisters telling me that I was the ugly one, who would have ugly babies. My mother did nothing to discourage the insults. In fact, I think she relished them.

I did everything I could to make myself just as beautiful as they were, but everything I did only made matters worse. I tried laying baby hair down. Okay, I have to admit it; I went into overkill with the baby hair. It was a hilarious sight. I would part what seemed like half my hair and lay it across my face with a huge gook of grease to lay it down since my hair was so thick. I was headed to school one morning with my gook laid baby hair and I asked my mother for the money to take my school photo. She said, "I'm not paying for nothing if you got that mess pasted to your face."

It's funny now, but boy did it hurt then. I didn't realize how ridiculous I looked. Here is the key to this point: If all the words that were thrown at me since I was old enough to understand their meaning weren't words of hate and discouragement, then maybe my mind and heart would have listened when they were words of encouragement or at least words that would head me in the right direction.

I was a child hated by family, friends, everyone, and if it wasn't for God dispatching His angels to keep watch over me, I doubt that I would have had the strength to be a strong Black woman today. The events in my life hardened me, they made me build a wall of protection and I believe they are the source of why parenting comes so hard for me.

If you asked me there was no just cause for the hatred, for the harsh words being thrown at me, the dead raccoon on my front door, the teasing, calling me Mr. T, and the laughing. As an adult I have come to understand people can only do to you what you allow. I harbored the harsh words from my home life so much that I had become to believe them and accept nothing more from my school life.

It is such a damaging ripple effect for a child to have to endure. As a child, you don't understand that you have the power to change your circumstance, so you feel hopeless and many times succumb to the only thing you feel is in your control, suicide.

Today, suicide is ranked as the third leading cause of death amongst children 5 – 14 years of age. We read about the loss in the papers and watch it on television. Our hearts feel the pain and devastation as we shake our heads and wonder what could a child so young have endured to make them want to end their lives.

We send our kids to school knowing that they are part of a growing epidemic. Whether they are the underdog or the bully, the one doing the damage or the one damaging, the bottom line says many of us aren't doing anything about it. We keep our situations within our home because we don't want others to know what we're going through or what we're putting our children through.

How healthy is it for the individual, especially when the result is a life lost that doesn't have to be? My childhood was filled with events that included having a knife put to my throat, being lifted by my womanhood and tossed across a room, kicked out of the home, ridiculed, and a phone thrown at me. These are just a few and these are just from my mother.

My father was ghost, he showed up just enough to let us know that he existed and he was alive. Yet, he would be the source to purchase my oldest sister and me the bike that my mother would not. He would also be the one to give us the only birthday party that I ever remember having as a child. Somehow those two events did not make up for his absence. That behavior continued into my adult life and the lives of his grandchildren.

In all that I have been through, I can stand now and say that He truly never puts more on you than you can bear. So as difficult as your situation seems while you're going through it, understand that He is only testing your strength and to make it through on the other side is a much better blessing than to give up on life.

Just as He dispatched His angels to watch over me, trust and know that they are watching over you to. Twenty something odd years would pass before I would look in the mirror and love the color of my skin and understand that God made me just as He saw fit and for that I am beautiful.

For me, ugly can only be defined by a person's character, not their looks. Do not let anyone make you feel anything but beautiful and that's including yourself. It is as the old adage so perfectly stated: beauty is in the eye of the beholder. So when you look at yourself in the mirror, behold your beauty.

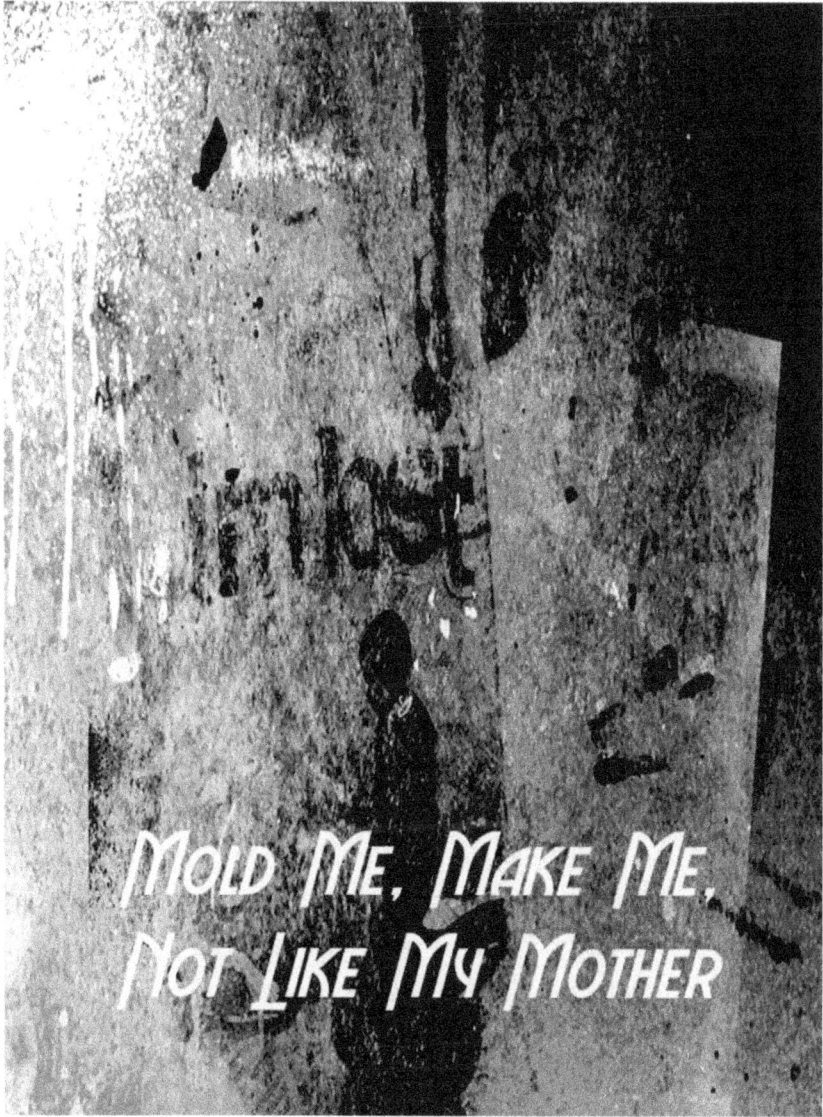

MOLD ME, MAKE ME,
NOT LIKE MY MOTHER

We were neighbors and the best of friends. Our apartments shared the same wall, so she heard everything that went on in my place and I heard everything in hers. We couldn't escape the other's turmoil if we wanted to.

"Say one more thing!" Nyah's mother yelled. I didn't hear Nyah say another thing, but I did hear the loud clash of flesh against flesh, and I knew that her mother had struck her again. I heard Nyah say something then as the sound of her crying enveloped my mind. I tried to place my hands over my ears to muffle out the sound that seemed like it would never go away.

BAM! The loud thud sounded against the same wall that my back was leaning on. The thin wall shook so hard I thought it had come from my apartment. I got up and ran across the room. I fell on my knees and rocked back and forth as I started praying. "Please make her stop, God. Please make her stop." I repeated over and over again.

The front door opened and slammed loudly. I went to my door and peeked out. I saw Nyah's mom heading down the hallway. I ducked my head back in just as she turned around. I wiped the beads of sweat off my head, glad that I hadn't got caught looking. Nyah's mom scared me. She was so pretty, tall and thin, but she scared me just the same. I didn't ever want her to catch me doing something bad, I didn't want her to hit me, too.

I rushed into the kitchen and made two peanut butter and jelly sandwiches. I opened the fridge and got two juice boxes and then I headed over to Nyah's. I knocked softly, she didn't answer. I tried the door and it opened. It always did. It was rare that I found it locked.

"Nyah," I cried out but she didn't answer. I walked to her bedroom and peeked in. "Nyah," I called again, but she still didn't answer. I was scared, I always was. I thought that one day I would find Nyah dead and I didn't know what I would do if I lost my best friend. I saw her foot on the floor of her bedroom closet. My heart started beating rapidly, but then the foot moved and I calmed down.

I ran to Nyah and sat next to her. She was crying and holding her baby sister Layla. Layla was four, while Nyah and I were both nine.

"She gone be right back, Tee Tee." Nyah said once she noticed that I was there.

"No she won't," I said confidently. "She never is." I watched Nyah's eyes grow big at the same time I felt her mother's presence hovering over me.

"You want to try that again," she said. I dropped the sandwiches and juice and high tailed it out of there. I wasn't sure if I would bump right into her when I turned around or not, it didn't matter. "That's right," I heard her call behind me. "You better get your fast tail on out of here. I'm gone tell your momma you was out, too."

I rushed into my apartment and shut the door. I couldn't fasten the locks quick enough. My heart was racing. She never came right back, never! I had to be more careful. I wondered if she would make good on her threat, because if momma knew I wasn't in the house, she would have my behind for sure.

It was dark when momma came home. I didn't know what time it was. I lay on my back looking straight up at the ceiling. I listened as her key turned in the lock, all the while praying that Nyah's momma wouldn't come out and say nothing. I didn't want no whipping.

When I heard momma come in and shut the door, I breathed. I didn't even know I was holding my breath the whole time. Momma came and shut the light on in my room. I closed my eyes fast. I shut them so tight that she knew I was playing possum.

"Ain't no sense in you over there pretending, Tee Tee. Gone head and get up out that bed," she said. I opened my eyes and saw the cigarette dangling from her lip and the belt hanging from her hand.

"Momma," I pleaded. "I just went to see if Nyah was okay. I didn't mean no harm."

"I told you to stay your little fast tail in the house," she said while making sure not to drop the cigarette to the floor. She took a long puff, and then put the cigarette out in the ashtray that sat on the table outside my room. "Come on," she said as if I was supposed to rush to my whipping.

"Momma, I just," I started before momma cut me off.

"I just nothing. I done told you 'bout leaving this house when I'm not home. You gone mess around and the wrong somebody gone see your little fast tail coming or going and then it's gone be too late. Now come on and get this butt whipping. If I have to come over there, it's gone be ten times worse."

I wanted to plead my case more. I wanted to tell her that if I was waiting for her to get home then I'd be waiting till the end of never, but that smart remark would have sent me straight to my maker fast. I climbed out the bed slowly and headed over to my mother for my beating.

Nyah was quiet on our walk to school the next day. I saw the huge bruise on her face and was surprised that she was coming to school at all. Normally, she would sit these days out until her face healed, or her arms, legs. The truancy officer had threatened to put a case on Nyah's mom, so I supposed that's why she was coming anyhow.

"Whatchu s'pose to say 'bout your face?" I asked as I looked toward the ground. I didn't want to look at Nyah. It was hard for me to see her face all beat up like that.

"I fell down the stairs while I was at my daddy's last night."

"Oh. Why you gotta say you was at your daddy's?"

"Cause, if they have some more questions, my mamma didn't want them to come round there asking her about it."

"So what happens when they ask your daddy?"

"They ain't ever gone find him. Shoot we have the toughest time finding him ourselves."

"Your momma thinks of everything, huh?"

"Yeah, I suppose. Tee Tee?"

"Huh."

"We friends, ain't we?"

"We best friends, Nyah. Why you ask that?"

"And best friends don't break promises, do they?"

"Of course they don't, Nyah."

"I want you to promise me that when we grow up, you make sure that I'm never gone be nothing like my momma."

"I promise, Nyah, but you got to promise me the same."

"I promise."

"Pinky swear."

"Pinky swear." And with that we linked our pinky fingers together and Nyah smiled for the first time that day.

Momma wasn't home when I got there, but dinner was on the stove. I went to the room and put my books away. I washed my hands and made my plate. Since momma wasn't home, I poured myself a big glass of grape Kool-Aid, even though I know I was only supposed to have a small glass. After I ate my dinner I put the food away and cleaned the kitchen.

I went back to the room and got my homework. I pulled out my books and got started. Nyah knocked on the door. I knew it was her because we had a special knock. Momma told me to never answer the door to nobody, so Nyah and I came up with a special knock, that way I would only go to the door when it was her.

"Hey," I said as I opened the door and let her and Layla in.

"Hey. Did your momma cook dinner tonight?" Nyah knew that she had. My momma always cooked dinner.

"Yeah, come on in."

I went and fixed Nyah and Layla a plate, then sat back down to finish my homework.

"When's your mom coming home?" Nyah asked.

"I don't know. How about yours?"

"I don't know either, but at least your mom left you with dinner."

"Yeah, I guess." I said unimpressed with my mom's attempt at parenting. I would rather have her home than a hot meal any day. I wouldn't complain though; I knew that Nyah was having a much harder go of it than I was.

"You're always doing your homework. You're probably the smartest girl in fourth grade."

"Probably, I make it my goal to succeed because I don't want to wind up like my mom."

"Neither do I," Nyah said as she stuffed a forkful of mashed potatoes in her mouth. "It's just; I always have Layla or something else going on. I don't have time for homework."

"You just have to make time, but if you don't, no worries. I'll make enough so that both of us can do better than our moms." At nine years old, Nyah was left to be a parent for a child that she never had. I shook my head at the sadness of it all, but right now there wasn't much more that I could do.

The alarm clock blaring on the side of my bed told me that it was time to get up and get ready for school. I stretched and opened my eyes before pressing the button to shut down the annoying alarm. I shot straight up when I noticed movement in the other twin bed across from mine. It was reserved for guest.

I rubbed the sleep from eyes, and calmed my nerves as I recognized the source behind the movement. Apparently, Nyah and Layla had slept over. Slept over! Oh no! I thought, if they slept over then that means that momma didn't come home last night. My feet hit the floor fast as I rushed to Nyah and began to shake her woke.

"Nyah, wake up," I urged as I continued to shake her from sleep to grogginess.

"Where's the fire?" she mumbled but I paid her no mind.

"The fire better be under your behind. Get up! It's time to get ready for school."

"School," Nyah said as she became more alert. "Wait a minute if it's a school day, then why am I here."

"Exactly," I said glad that she was finally making sense of this. She woke Layla up and they went to their apartment. I went to my mother's room only to find that she hadn't made it home. It wouldn't be the first time, but that didn't stop me from worrying every time she didn't.

I went to the bathroom to get ready for school. When I came out of my room, dressed and ready to go, my momma had made it home. She sat at the dining room table smoking a cigarette as if nothing was wrong. I didn't make her think otherwise. I grabbed my book bag and headed toward the door.

"You look like a slut," she bellowed.

I looked down at my attire. I wore Levi blue jeans, Adidas gym shoes with an Adidas jersey, my lips were glossed lightly. I didn't see what she saw, but I was not one to argue.

"Thank you," I mumbled as I walked out the door. Nyah was exiting her apartment too. She still had Layla which meant we had to drop her off at Mrs. Johnson's before heading to school.

"Your momma still ain't home?"

"No," she said as she hung her head low. "Yours?"

"Yeah, she's in there."

"She's still not home?" I asked Nyah as I helped her load their clothes in the washer.

"No, and Mrs. Johnson is startin' to get suspicious."

"It's been two weeks!"

"The gas went off last week; we ain't had a phone in a while, now the lights is off too. If it wasn't for you, we wouldn't even have nothing to eat. I keep telling Mrs. Johnson that momma says she coming with her money, but she don't seem like she believe me no more."

"Nyah, what is you gone do?" I asked, my heart breaking. Nyah's situation was far worse than mine. I didn't like my situation either, but hers made me glad that I didn't have to live the way she was.

"I 'on't know. I guess I'll just call my dad."

"I thought you ain't know how to reach him."

"I do, I just don't let my momma know. She always harassing him for money and calling him all kinds of names, so I talks to him when she's not around."

"Oh," I said both happy and sad at the knowledge. I didn't want Nyah to go live with her dad, but I was glad that she had another option. "Why don't you give it a day or two then call him? Maybe your mom will come home. My mom's never here, you and Layla can stay with me; she won't even know."

"I suppose I can do that," Nyah said as she smiled with sad eyes, and I knew that she was breaking up inside.

Nyah's mom didn't come home. She had given it another week, to no avail. She called her Dad; he was furious that she hadn't called earlier. He came to pick them up, making sure that he paid Mrs. Johnson for her time and services. I watched at the door as Nyah walked away from her apartment door for the last time. She turned around and waved bye; I forced my hand up to do the same as the tears rolled quietly down my face.

Two weeks later there was a new family moving in, they had children around my age, too. I wasn't going to be friends with them though; I didn't want to attach myself to nobody else. I couldn't do it. My heart couldn't do it.

"Nyah?" I said excitement all over my face. It had been fifteen years since I had seen her. I never forgot about her, always thinking about her, wondering if she was making out okay. Now she was standing right in front of me and I was as happy as I could be.

"Tee-Tee?" she asked in reply as she walked closer to me, tears threatening to fall. "Oh my God, I can't believe it's really you."

I hugged her tightly.

"Yes, but I go by Tiana now," I said releasing our embrace. "I knew you would grow up to be so beautiful."

"You didn't do so bad yourself, Tee-Tee. I mean, Tiana. You gone have to give me a minute on that one."

"It's fine," I said noticing the diamond ring. "You're married now?"

"Girl, yes, and he's so good to me."

She had found happiness and it was so good to see.

"You deserve it, Nyah. How's Layla?"

"She doing well; she's over at Clark Atlanta doing her thing?"

"Oh wow, that's so wonderful. So, I guess it turned out to be good that things worked out that way." I choked the words out, I didn't want to broach the subject but I was burning to know from the time that Nyah left that door.

"Our lives got better, I mean, we never had to worry about food, the lights, and the gas. Our dad came home at night, but to tell you the truth Tee-Tee, I still can't get over the fact that my mom abandoned us. I mean she really just got up and decided that she wasn't coming back.'

"Have you heard from her anymore?" I asked as she and I walked over and sat on a bench nearby. Our "catching-up" was going to take some time.

"Yeah, she called when I was around seventeen. She wanted to come to my graduation."

"Did she come?"

"She was there, but Tee-Tee, I wasn't ready to see her. I was so mad at her."

"Yeah, but Nyah, you got to go to a better place."

"I would have rather stayed then to have this feeling of abandonment that I have. When she beat me, I felt something, but when she left me, there was nothing left to feel. I was empty. Every time I meet somebody now, I don't never let them get too close 'cause I'm always afraid that they gone leave, just like she did. You don't know what that does to a child. It's not an easy thing to get over."

"So what are you supposed to do?"

"Keep living, keep loving, keep understanding. I have to be extra cautious with my daughter now, because I don't ever want her to feel the way I do."

"You have a daughter?"

"I do," she said as she flipped through her phone, and then turned it toward me so I could see her daughter.

"She's beautiful, Nyah."

"Thank you, that's exactly how I want her to stay, too. Once you become damaged emotionally, it's hard to regain that beauty."

I listened to her speak; I had my answers. She had her pain, and in all that she said, I understood this: She was a long way from healing. Though the physical scars had healed, the emotional and mental ones were still open wounds.

On The Battlefield

He was wise beyond his years. If I had half the wisdom as he then I wouldn't have made the mistakes that I have. I would admit to the ones that I make, but I wasn't as wise, so I let the wounds and scars that I had placed on him emotionally and physically fester. They festered until he no longer cared. I was his mother, but that was in title only.

"Suspended! Again! Come on now, seriously!" I looked at Andru angrily. Suspensions were becoming second nature for him and it was working my last nerve while he just blew it off.

"I just needed a break," Andru said calmly.

"So you get suspended?" I asked in utter disbelief.

"If I told you that I wanted to stay home for a few days, that I just needed some time to clear my head, would you have let me stay?"

"No," I said looking at him like he was crazy.

"Exactly, so I got suspended. Mr. Mitchell was making it hard. He didn't want to suspend me either, but he finally gave in." He walked away.

"Dru," I said not done with the conversation. He stopped, turned and looked at me. "We're not done."

"Yes we are," he said calmly as he continued to his room.

Now, I was furious. Dru and I were constantly butting heads and I was getting past fed up with it. The fact that he thought he had the upper hand in our conversations was really beginning to get under my skin.

Our neighbors were coming for dinner; I didn't have the time to argue with him, nor did I care to. I hurried and made the last minute preparations. I greeted them at the door with a smile plastered to my face. I was no longer in the mood to pretend that things were "peachy" when everything in me was a ball of confusion, a world of emotions.

Diane saw right through the smile as she rubbed my arm lightly, "What's wrong?"

"Everything and nothing," I said as I took their coats.

Robert made it down the stairs as if on cue. I was glad; I wasn't ready to greet the Evans' on my own. "What it do?" he said as he went and shook Mike's hand.

"You, got it," Mike said as they pushed their chest up on the other.

Our dinner conversation touched on many topics of interest from politics to religion, yet none of it took my mind off of Dru. Something needed to change in our household and I didn't know where to begin. I was thinking of just going to court and filing him as incorrigible.

"Yvette, you keep saying nothing is wrong, but I can tell all over your face that something is weighing heavy on your mind. What's really going on?"

"I don't know, Diane. I guess it's just Dru. I'm still having issues with him and I don't know what else to do. I think I'm going down to the court tomorrow and just letting go."

Mike looked at me wide-eyed; he and I rarely spoke to one another. The Evans family was wonderful and they offered such great advice, but my conversation was usually with Diane, even in settings like these. He was on the police force and I knew he had dealt with his share of bad seeds. His interest was piqued; I was glad. They had children of their own and yet, their world seemed so perfect while mine seemed to be falling apart at the seams.

I didn't envy them though; I was just happy for them and glad that there were Black families that could actually be successful at love, life and all of the trials and tribulations it brought.

"So, what's going on?" Mike said as he wiped his mouth with the napkin, slid his plate from in front of him and crossed his arms.

I told them about Dru and the issues that I was having with him and his disrespect. They nodded and listened intently. I was glad for the listening ear and anxious to hear what their opinion would be at the close of my spiel.

"Everyone has issues; teens are no different from adults. Not one of us is perfect," Mike began, and I frowned at the revelation, that wasn't what I was preparing myself to hear.

"Andru is a pretty good kid. I watch him; I listen to how respectful he is. Trust me, in my line of work you see some bad kids. Andru isn't one of them." I began to feel a little relieved, but at the same time I knew that Dru was giving me too many issues and I didn't want to just sweep it under the rug.

"Let me ask you this," Mike said. "Does he do drugs?"

"No," Robert and I both said together.

"Is he selling them?"

"Not to our knowledge," Robert said. I shook my head, agreeing with Robert's statement.

"Is he being physical with either of you? Is he abusive?"

"No, it's not that, it's just, I don't know," I said as the problems that I was having with Dru seemed to be minimal now.

"Listen to me closely," Mike said. "You do not want to put him in the system unnecessarily, because I can promise you this, his problems will not get better. They will only get worse. You're putting a good kid in there with boys who are really from the street and live by it. That's no place for him."

"Not to mention the abandonment issues that he would be having," Diane added.

"Exactly," Mike agreed as he nodded his head in her direction.

"So what do you suggest?" I asked earnestly needing some reprieve.

"Have you tried counseling?" Diane asked.

I looked at Robert, now my eyes were wide as I thought, *Why would she even suggest that?*

"No, we haven't," I said as I turned my head back to Diane in disbelief.

Dru's timing was impeccable as he came in and spoke to the Evans' on his way to the kitchen for a plate.

"Come have a seat when you're done," I said to him. I knew that he didn't too much care for the Evans' but I also knew that he wouldn't be downright disrespectful either. When he sat down, I gave him an overview of the conversation that we had just had with the Evans'. He looked at me as if I was crossing the line; I shrugged my shoulders back at him to let him know he was leaving me little choice.

"So," Mike said. "What's going on with you, Man?"

"Nothing," Dru said shrugging his shoulders.

"So why are you and your mom having so many problems?"

"I don't have any problems; she seems to think that I do."

Diane and Mike both looked at me; I smiled smugly as I saw that they were getting the gist of my point.

"Okay," I said confident that the conversation was going to go my way. "We have an issue with his Facebook page. He wouldn't friend me, so I had discontinued his computer use until he did."

"That's good," Diane said. Mike nodded as he continued to listen. Robert sat quietly, already knowing the history. Dru looked down at the table; I shifted in my seat and continued.

"Well he friended me, but then he blocked me from so much, it wasn't even worth him friending me."

"You kept commenting on everything," Dru said in explanation.

"That's what she's supposed to do," Diane said.

"No, she's not. That's my page, she's supposed to respect my privacy and let me have a place to vent."

I looked over at Diane and Mike trying to gage their reactions; they looked appalled. I shifted in my seat again, doing the *ummm humph* nod, my lips turned up.

The conversation went for a half an hour or better, going over little small things that I had issues with Dru about. Dru sat patiently listening, commenting when necessary, each time burying him deeper as the Evans' eyes grew more sympathetic for me by the moment.

After Dru left the table, Diane looked back at me and again said, "Yeah, maybe you should really consider counseling."

I did seek counseling for Dru and I. The first sessions were mundane, he and I both sitting there, arms crossed, refusing to take responsibility for the state of our relationship. Him saying it's me, I'm saying it's him. After three sessions, I was ready to call it quits. A light bulb came on and that's when I knew I had to give it a fighting chance.

I went to a poem that Dru had written and read it over. It said so much. I brought it with me to our next session. I handed it to the psychologist and gave her a few minutes to digest its content.

"Do you still feel this way?" she asked Dru.

"I don't know; I guess so," he answered.

"Do you trust your mother?"

"No."

"So then the answer is not, 'you guess so,' it's no."

"Then, no."

"What has she done to not have your trust?"

"I don't know."

She looked at me for an answer. I gave her one. "Dru will not forgive me for the time when my live-in boyfriend abused him, and then when my husband tried to discipline him, he considers that as abuse as well."

"It is abuse," Dru said. "She's not even trying to take her responsibility in it. He put his hands around my throat, that's abuse, but not just him. You did, you choked me, and you punched me in my chest, numerous times. You kicked me out of the house."

Progress was being made, my feet felt cemented to the ground, my throat was dry, my wall tried to go back up so that I could cower and hide behind it. Truth lay in his every word. I never identified any of that as abuse and now I see him, I see his words, and I know the depth of the pain that I have caused. I can't speak, there are no words. I wouldn't know what to say if I could form them.

"You're not the only parent that has wanted to put their hands around their kids' throat and choke the daylights out of them, but there are few who actually do," she began and I listened in a hardened stance.

"If child protective services were ever called on any of these events they would be hard pressed not to find what you did as abuse. There is a thin line, well," she said as she pondered on her thoughts, "yeah; we'll go with thin line between what is abuse and what is discipline. I suggest that you do no more physical discipline."

He was now sixteen, the physical discipline had stopped long ago, but the hurt and pain remained. Our session ended.

I walked out feeling a heavier load on my shoulder, but with the understanding that he had been carrying a heavier load for years. He tried to tell me that I abused him, but I didn't want to hear him; all I heard was an unruly child refusing discipline. He came into this world with so much love ready to give and ready to receive and because I couldn't see him for who he was, I missed out on the time that I could have enjoyed him for who he was.

I encourage you, when your children speak, listen to them. My son has gone through so much which inadvertently has made him put others through so much. It wasn't his fault. He was acting out from what I refused to see. In his youth he has been blessed with wisdom. Take the time to understand your children. Don't make the assumption for the worse; a life is in your hands. What will you do with it?

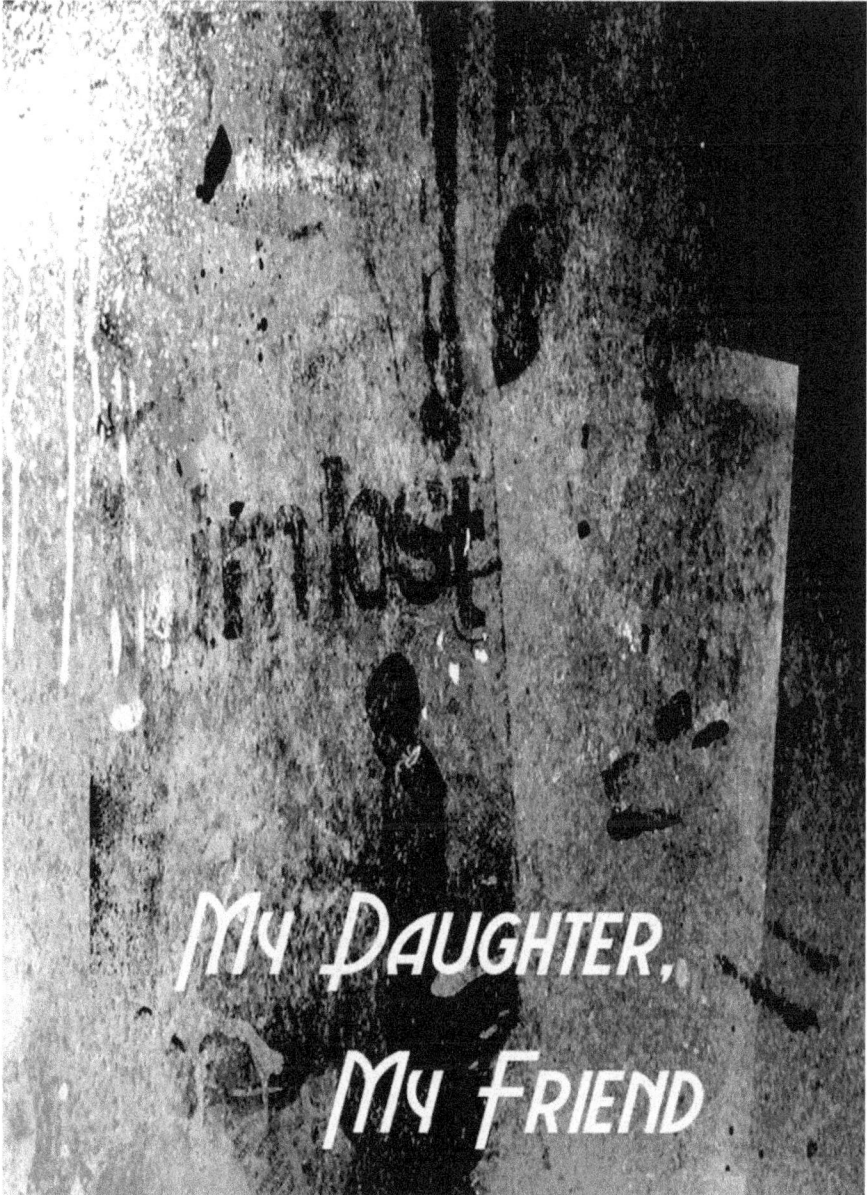

My Daughter, My Friend

Written by L. Smith and Norlita Brown

It was unbearably loud, my head was throbbing. I placed my hands over my ears, but the noise wouldn't leave me.

"Mommy's on the floor," I shouted as I ran to the room and peered in at my mother lying flat on the floor. "Daddy," I screamed as I pulled at my father's pant leg. "Get mommy off the floor!"

Staff from nurses to aides, maybe a few doctors, doctors who had just left to get a drink and it wasn't no soda. I smelled the liquor on their breath as everyone ran to my mother and lifted her off the floor.

Tears were running down my face, landing on my new black and white shoes. Somehow the tears made their way to the top of my head. I felt them falling, I thought maybe it was rain, until I realized we were inside. It doesn't rain in the hospital does it? I looked up and saw my father was matching my tears with ones of his own. He held my brother tight in one arm. He had just left this room; she was fine when he left. He just wanted to come home and get us, now it was too late. Mommy was dead and there was nothing we could do about it.

The banging started again, doors were slamming, and pots were clanging. I ran back to the room, maybe Mommy was still alive. Maybe it was just a bad dream. As hard as I tried to get back to the room, I couldn't. Someone or something was holding me back. "Let me go!" I shouted as I tried tirelessly to snatch myself free.

"Stop it daddy," I yelled. "Let me go," I repeated.

"I'm not your daddy," the voice said as I looked at the hand that clenched mine so tightly. It wasn't daddy's, it was soft, it was my auntie's hand. "Auntie," I said softly, giving up the fight, I looked up into the face of my grandmother.

The banging continued, the slamming grew louder, I tossed and I turned until the noise was so unbearable it shook me from the nightmare that continued to force me to look at my childhood; continued to remind me that my mother was gone. My daddy raised me the best he could with the help of my grandmother and my aunt. They were so strict I felt like I couldn't breathe. It was the same feeling that was overcoming me now.

I sat straight up in my bed covered in sweat listening to the noise that wouldn't stop. Tanisha was at it again. She must have had another argument with Tyrone. I went from one nightmare to another and I wasn't sure when either would end.

I dragged myself from the bed and made my way to the kitchen where Tanisha still remained banging dishes around in her attempt to clean them.

"What in the world is going on now?" I asked as I looked around noticing that there wasn't that many dishes so there was no need for the unwanted off key musical that she decided to give me.

"Nothin'" Tanisha said as she slammed the pot down on the counter.

"Tanisha, my head can't take another unnecessary noise. It's quite obvious something's wrong."

"You asked me to do the dishes, I'm doing them."

"It don't take all of that, Tanisha. Besides, I asked you to do them yesterday; you're just now getting to them?" I asked as I walked over to the cabinet pulling down a glass.

"I was busy!"

"You ain't doing nothing," I said in amazement as I made my way to the fridge and poured a glass of orange juice. "You and Tyrone been sitting up under me, rent free for over a year. You think I don't know y'all selling just as much weed as you're smoking up in my house?"

"Whatever," she said making no attempt to mumble it under her breath. She was getting way beside herself. Nineteen years old and I was ready to smack the living mess out of her.

Tyrone is Tanisha's live-in boyfriend of five years. That's right, you read correct, there is no typo. Five years, I'll say it again while you do the math in your head. In fact I'll help you out. Tanisha was fourteen years old when I let Tyrone move in.

When I was young, I used to get in trouble for everything under the sun, even when it wasn't true, I was always guilty. One of my Aunties that watched us a lot used to call us in from outside just to go in the kitchen to get her some water or bring her the TV remote that wasn't even ten steps away from where she was sitting. As a little girl I made a promise to myself that if and when I had kids, first, I wouldn't use them as slaves; second, I won't gone whip them about every little thing, and I won't believe everyone except them, and finally, I would be their best friend. On April 29, 1991, God gave me my first born, Tanisha. By the time she was six months, that little girl had a gold chain, a gold bracelet, the newest Jordan's out at the time, little miniature grown up clothes. I mean, from birth she had all top notch things; I wanted her to never accept less, because I never had any of those things.

Tanisha was allowed to pick out the clothes she wanted to wear as young as elementary school. If I picked what she didn't like, she would cry and throw a temper tantrum, so it was her way or no way. She got anything she asked for that was financially in my means. My ex-husband's mother made a statement to me one day, "You think you're doing right by her, but one day that girl is gonna hurt you bad and make you cry." I thought, *What is she talking about I'm an excellent mother, my daughter gonna love me dearly forever.*

All of Tanisha's young life there wasn't much that she wanted that she didn't get, even now its name brand or nothing. I convinced myself that I would be the kind of mother that my daughter would come to when anything was going wrong; she wouldn't be afraid of getting in trouble over me helping her with her problem. I called myself setting it up to end up just like that, me being her very best FRIEND.

At the age of twelve is when she started liking boys and instead of me saying, "Girl you're too young to be liking boys, get your mind on them books and make something of yourself so that you won't need a man to take care of you financially when you get older. It will be a choice to have a husband not a need!" I was too busy trying to be a friend, so instead I catered to her new found fondness of boys and began commenting on whether they were cute or not. My apartment was the hangout spot. It was nothing for me to wake up to about ten boys and girls asleep in my living room, not cuddled together or anything like that, just crashed from playing video games, dancing, playing music, and eating up all the food all night.

Tanisha used to tell me all the time, "Mom, all my friends like you; they say you're the coolest mom they know. They said their moms are mean and don't let them have company late at night, and no boys at all, and they have a lot of chores to do. They're not nice like you."

At that point in time, I was dumb enough to actually take that as a compliment. Trying so hard to fight against the upbringing I had; trying to give my children the exact opposite, I gave them something far worse.

It was summer 2005, right around the time of the tragedy in New Orleans. Tanisha, who was now fourteen years old had developed an "I'm above everything and how dare you ask me to clean or pick up after myself" attitude.

We temporarily moved into an extended stay hotel while I found a house to buy. It was the last month we were there while we were waiting out the thirty days needed to close on the house I was buying. While going into our room, this young guy that lived two doors down with his mother and sisters waked by, and I stated, "He's a real cutie pie isn't he?" Why did I say that? She may have never noticed him if had I kept my "Ms. trying to be cool" mouth shut.

A couple days later I happened to be outside started talking to the cute boy's mother's boyfriend. I stated how my fourteen year old daughter was ready to move because it was so boring over here, not being around her friends and not having anything to do. He stated his girlfriend's son was the same age and was making the same complaints. I assume he went and told the boy about my daughter 'cause and hour later the boy came and knocked on the door, introducing himself as Tyrone Cook.

He was very respectful and polite; he asked could my daughter come outside and just hang out and talk. I said yes, of course. Little did I know that was the beginning of the end of my baby girl's childhood. Tanisha and Tyrone started hanging together every day, but I wasn't worried. I thought to myself they're not interested in having sex or anything because they're so young and my daughter acts like a big Tom boy, always wrestling and playing all rough.

About two weeks later Tyrone and his family moved to another extended stay directly next to the one we were in. Now, my daughter was never home; she was always with him at their room because they had a pool. A week later, Tanisha called my cell while I was working, crying and saying that Tyrone's family was gonna be separated because Red Cross wasn't paying for their room anymore. She told me that his mother couldn't find work and had no money and all of the shelters that weren't filled with New

Orleans survivors only accepted females, no males. This meant he would be separated from his family. She begged me to help them. Here again, different title same stupidity, I had now moved to being "Miss Trying to Save the World." I told Tanisha to let me talk to Tyrone's mom, Barbra. Barbara told me that they were on the top of the waiting list for government housing and would be placed very soon. I, in turn, told her to get their belongings since they had to leave that room and go to my room. I agreed to take care of it when I got off work.

A few hours later, I got money from the bank and went and paid $200.00 for them to stay at the room for another week. Barbra and I started talking a lot; she was a nice lady, trying her best who had just hit hard times. I was buying a four bedroom home with two more rooms in the basement that could be bedrooms. I told her that if the housing hadn't come through for them by the time I closed on my house and moved from the extended stay, that they were welcome to move with me until housing came through for them.

I felt so good inside 'cause I had convinced myself that I was doing such a good thing, helping a family in need. Deep inside I knew that if Tanisha didn't like this boy and wouldn't cry like her like her world was ending, I would have said goodbye and take care to Tyrone and his family. I would have moved into my home and let them make it the best way they could. November 2005 arrived, bringing with it the day I closed on my big home. As promised, I took Barbra, Tyrone and family with me. Barbra moved into the basement and me and the kids stayed in the main part of the home. When I would ask Barbra what the housing people were saying about their housing status, she said that all the New Orleans people got priority on the available places to live, and that the rest were put on the back burner so they didn't have a clue when they could find them a place to go. I told her, "Girl, don't worry about it. As you can see I have plenty of room."

I later found out that Tyrone was in a gang. I thought, *Wow, I picked the worse guy for my daughter to talk to.* I was blinded by the fact that he was so nice and polite in front of me. I thought he was the perfect little gentleman. Everyone had separate rooms, but since Tanisha and Tyrone couldn't be together, their slick behinds would fall asleep together in the living room; one on the sofa and the other on the floor right next to the sofa.

Once again I thought to myself the way these two are always wrestling and playing Xbox like two boys, they're not doing anything sexual, wishful thinking on my part. I was always working long hours and lots of over time; I needed it. I had a lot of responsibilities now, caring for a second family.

I was never around and when things would go wrong at home and the kids would fight, I asked Barbra why she didn't come upstairs and regulate. She said to me, "I don't get in the kids business." I was so pissed. What kind of business could a kid have? Only a horrible mother would say she don't get in it, so me and Barbra fell out about that.

I was already regretting taking Tyrone's family in and it hadn't even been thirty days yet.

December came around and Tanisha came to me saying, "Mom, it hurts so bad when I urinate." I went to the drug store and got some stuff that says it helped and some cranberry juice since she didn't mention anything else. I figured that was all that was wrong, I was being cheap, as I thought, *I'm not going to the doctor with a $20 copay when I can get some cheaper stuff for her*. Fortunately it didn't work or I would have never found out what Tanisha wasn't telling me.

About mid-December, I took Tanisha to the doctor and he suggested doing a pap smear and pregnancy test. I said, "Okay, whatever you think is best; you're the doctor," but I thought, *Isn't she kind of young for a pap?* I didn't know that as soon as a young lady starts her cycle, she should get a pap smear from then on.

Anyway, the doctor comes in after the pap and says, "Your daughter has so much infection up in her tubes and ovaries that I can't believe you just now brought her in!"

I told him, "I couldn't have known what she was going through until she came to me."

He ignored my response; I'm sure thinking that I was quite unfit, as he looked back at his chart and replied, "She will need two shots and medicine."

We waited for him to come back in with the prescription, but not only did he come back with the prescription, he came back with news that placed my bottom lip to the floor and my heart underneath my foot.

He came in and said, "I have something else to tell you. Tanisha's pregnant."

I thought my heart would stop beating I was so shocked and disappointed, not in her, but myself 'cause I knew this was my fault. I called Barbara to tell her and she asked, "What are we gonna do?" I thought, *We? This is going to be on me. You don't have any money to help one way or the other.'*

I decided quickly that I wasn't letting my fourteen year old have a baby. I knew that my job's insurance paid for abortions, so in my mind it was already decided. Tyrone and Tanisha got together as if I asked their opinion and decided that they wanted to keep the baby. Tanisha was talking about how Tyrone would get a part time job and go to school, and she would stop going to school as long as she could go back after the baby. I almost cursed those kids out, but I didn't.

I took a couple deep breaths then told Tanisha, "Do you know how much it costs to take care of a baby? A part time job won't even pay for the daycare. I have to work long hours and I'm barely taking care of all six of us. The gas bill runs $300, plus the electric is $250, plus the mortgage is $1300 a month. I can't afford to pay $125 or more for daycare while you two go to school and I go to work. You know his mom isn't gonna baby sit. You and Tyrone are still kids yourselves; you're not even mature enough to know that something is wrong with your body. You didn't know having a smelly discharge is a sign of infection, so you're not as grown as you like to think you are."

Monday came and it was off to school for Tanisha and Tyrone. About two hours after they had gone, I got a call from the school telling me that I needed to go up there. I go up there and it turned out that Tanisha went to school crying to a counselor that she was pregnant and I was forcing her to get an abortion. Anger didn't begin to describe how I felt with her putting the school in our home business.

The counselor said she had no choice but to call the children protective services because of Tanisha's age. She also warned me that they would be coming to my home to investigate the living conditions and the age of the father to make sure it wasn't an adult male there that could have gotten her pregnant. We had to tell her who the father was and admit that he was also a fourteen year old student there. Fortunately, we were never investigated. I found out that the age of the father it wasn't a legal matter because he was also a minor, thank God.

December 22, 2005, Tanisha got the abortion against her will. Both the kids hated me for a while but I didn't give a care. After Tanisha saw how her sixteen year old stepsister was having a hard time with her baby, and the daddy did not want to be with her after the baby came, she was glad I didn't let her have the baby. Tanisha was able to finish school baby-free. I was happy about that even though I had a sick feeling inside, knowing that her body had to go through that kind of physical trauma because of me being a friend, not a mother. I should have not allowed Tyrone to live in my home with her knowing one day they would be sexual. I knew inside that I officially earned the Worse Mother of the Year Award in 2005.

Tanisha and Tyrone are still living together in my home as of June 2010. The rest of his family went back to South Carolina. The young couple still play and wrestle like little children although they are both nineteen now. When they're not playing, they fight like cats and dogs and I know that she's not truly happy. My youngest daughter told me that she told her that her life is all messed up and to never get a boyfriend.

Tanisha has so much rage inside her that when she gets mad, she throws things and slams things, and when she cries real hard she has anxiety attacks. She stands outside and screams to the top of her lungs. One of my neighbors called the police 'cause he thought someone was killing her, but every time I mention putting him out, she threatens to kill herself and says he will be homeless again and has nowhere to go.

My poor baby is so messed up inside that if I say no to anything she wants, I get doors being slammed and dishes being slammed down extra hard to make sure I hear it all the way in my room from the kitchen. I try my best not to get mad and go off on her 'cause I know this is the monster inside of her that I created, so I just suck it in and deal with it.

I feel like I'm being controlled by a teen, but how dare I have a problem with it now? I didn't for eighteen years, right? I blame myself every day because I took away my baby's childhood and at the age of fourteen made her a grown up with a live-in boyfriend. Now they're like an old married couple. She didn't get to hang out with her friends and go places, and do things that I did as a normal teen because I had a grandmother that raised me after my mother died at the age of twenty who didn't play, not even a little bit. I wish I could have been like that.

Tanisha should not know the kind of pain and rage that she has inside herself, but thanks to me trying to be a friend and make her happy at all costs, I cost her a life of physical and emotional pain. I can't prove it, but I know he hits her when they fight 'cause I'm an ex-battered woman myself and I recognize the signs even without seeing physical bruises.

I made her grow up way too early and now she will probably before long need professional help for her rage and temper issues. Tanisha is 19, won't clean up, gets high everyday all day with Tyrone, and drinks alcohol with him. As I have mentioned before, Tyrone sells weed out of my place and they think I don't know. They won't try to find jobs or do anything for themselves. This is what you get if you try to be your child's friend and not their parent.

The noise has started again, the banging, the slamming is constant. My head hits the concrete hard; my face is trickling with the blood from his first blow. I didn't make dinner fast enough, he said. I feel my eye swelling, I want to reach and touch it, but I can't. I have to use my hands to balance myself as he drags me by my feet up the concrete stairs.

It is my fault, I tried to run; if I had stayed in the house then I wouldn't be feeling the pain of my head hitting each concrete step. There are six, our porch has six cold, hard concrete steps and as hard as I try to balance myself to prevent my head from hitting it, I am unsuccessful. I feel the blows; I wonder what the neighbors are thinking. There is no way that I will survive this. I prayed that someone would call the police.

He was yelling something. I couldn't concentrate on his words, finally the steps were over; I felt like I was going in and out of consciousness. He has to stop! He doesn't. As soon as he has pulled and dragged my body into the home, his fists meet every part of my body. There is no mercy, no love. *How did I get myself into a situation like this?* I think, as I give up the fight and slowly allow my mind to drift into peacefulness. I am now sleep, the nightmare is now over.

The slamming continues. I jump; I am now awake again. I touch my head to wipe the blood away. I look, it is only sweat. I have just relived another horrible day in my life. Again, I make my way to the kitchen, Tanisha is at it again. This time the bruise on her eye confirms my suspicions. Tyrone is beating her.

"What happened?" I ask, although I really didn't want the details. It was too much for me. I knew that nothing would change. She would still be with him; I wouldn't put him out of the house. She still wouldn't want me to.

"He found out about Michael," she said as fresh tears appeared, quickly flowing down her cheeks.

"Who is Michael?" I drug the words out. Tanisha had been missing in action a lot lately. I feared that this was the case, and at the same time, I hoped that it was. She needed to be set free from Tyrone and maybe, just maybe, another man is what it would take.

"A guy I have been seeing."

"For how long?"

"A year."

"Then you got what you deserved," I said surprised at my own words as shock filled my daughter's face. I had ruined her and I was sorry. When she would find out the truth in those words, I don't know. I walked away, leaving her where she stood.

www.ingramcontent.com/pod-product-compliance
Lightning Source LLC
Chambersburg PA
CBHW051811040426
42446CB00007B/620